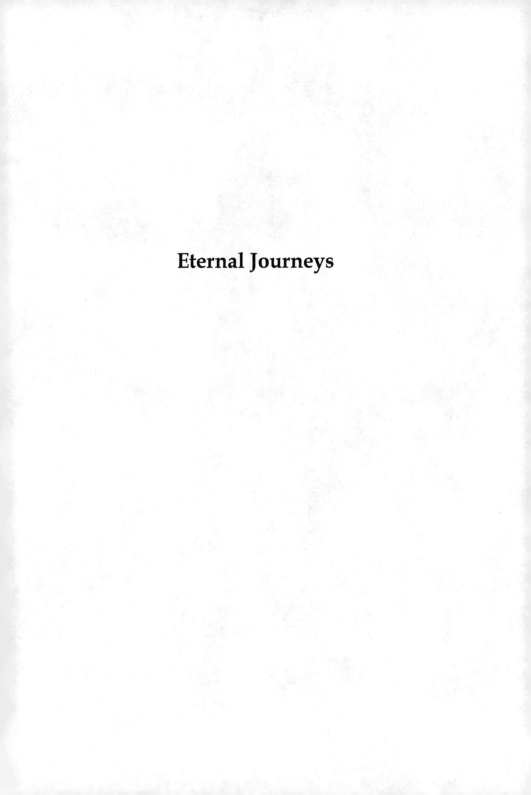

Eternal Journeys

Walid Touma

Eternal Journeys

Olympia Publishers
London

www.olympiapublishers.com
OLYMPIA HARDBACK EDITION

A CIP catalogue record for this title is
available from the British Library.

ISBN: 978-1-78830-831-1

The information in this book has been compiled by way of general
guidance only. Neither the author nor the publisher shall be liable or
responsible for any loss or damage allegedly arising from any
information or suggestion in this book.

First Published in 2021

Olympia Publishers
Tallis House
2 Tallis Street
London
EC4Y 0AB
Printed in Great Britain

Dedication

To Rania, My Eternal…

Contents

Prologue

My existential writings are about opening eyes, prodding one to enquire, to ask questions, to find answers… They are about a journey of enlightenment, of discovery, of self-awareness and acceptance…

Eternal Journeys captures moments in life, moments of introspection, of calmness, of peace, of rage and fury. Such moments, my moments, are all immersed with the will to share my existential struggle with a phenomenological approach, albeit in a minimalist way, but with the eternal screams of a terminal and vulnerable human being, a slowly vanishing dot in life…

I do hope that all the shared moments are enough to push the boundaries of both my spirit and yours, to transform our life and transcend our predicament… or better yet, to bow in peace and just be…

Enjoy the journey…

WALID R. TOUMA, PhD
Beirut, Lebanon
2021

Preface

Time

Time…
Dances around me like a thief…
Plays with me like a cheap toy…
Steals my life…
Robs me of my inner peace…
Knocks me around like worn out shoes…
Tortures me mercilessly, with no remorse, no compassion…
Forgets me by the wayside…
Tickles me, not caring for my falling tears…
Awakens me from my forgetfulness, my intentional
ignorance…
Makes me weep for memories…
Depletes me from moments past…
Eliminates me from time…
Abuses my faith in eternity…
Molests my innocence of being…
Screams at me in utter silence…
Calls on me silently to my guillotine…
Kills me slowly…

Time, my eternal companion…
I know you exist because I am, still…
I know you exist because I exist, still…
I know you are because I can be, still…
I know you need me for you to exist…for now…
I know you so well, I threw away my watch…
I know you will be by my side no matter what… as if I had a choice…
I know you are… and…
I know I am… for now… and for a while, I hope…

Time, my 'faithful' friend…
Allow me to stay with you, around you, near you…
Allow me… as long as possible…

You know well I am a loyal friend… or so I pretend…
You know well I don't have a choice… and that we both know…
You know well both you and our 'friend' death will win in the end…
You know well you will stay beyond me…

O Time…
I do hope you will preserve my memory…
I do hope you will retell my journey…
I do hope you will remember me after I am long gone…
I do hope you will allow me to be your eternal friend, watching, observing, in awe of your absolute power over eternity…

O Time… My Time…
O Master of eternal journeys…
O Gatekeeper of eternity…
O Eternal friend…
O Merciless…
O Brutal…
O…

Creative Relativity

Smile

When I look around me, ponder over long-gone experiences, dive through my deep-seated memories, my moments... I smile...

When I stop to question why certain harsh events are taking place in my life today, I find myself resenting some, feeling perplexed by others, or flat out rejecting and resisting even the mere thought of yet others... And when a few hours, days, months pass since I first stopped to think about such events, and I look back again... back to that moment in time... I smile...

Impatient with today, with the moment, one can easily miss the sweet answers tomorrow will bring... And when tomorrow is here, there are already new events unfolding and stopping us, and so on... However, when we stop and look back at what it was that was really bothering us on that particular day in the past, and consider it today, reflect on it today, perceive it through the light of the present moment, we smile... a smile born of recognition that its initial potency and undesired impact is diminished simply because we can look back at it...

Moreover, impatient with today, one can easily miss the solid answers our past holds, the ricochets and repercussions of our past actions and how they unfold today, in our lives, in direct manifestations, inflicted upon us as a result of our past, our long-gone actions, and the effect of which is affirming itself today...

Karma

Karma, originating from Indian and Chinese religions such as Hinduism, Buddhism, and Taoism, among others, has filtered itself in the common psyche of both eastern and western countries. The foundation of karma rests on how an individual's current actions influence her/his future in the form of manifested consequences, be they good or bad, in direct response to actions perpetrated by the individual in the cycle of time, the cycle of history.

The cycle of time, or the karmic cycle, can be a solid foundation for deterrence and discipline within societies. Nevertheless, the power of karma is that it manifests itself in the future of an individual in her/his current life; moreover, in Indian religions, karma can also manifest itself in future lives, rebirths, and reincarnations (*samsara*). As such, karmic cycles will be borne by the individual, her/his reincarnated spirit, if any, and that of her/his offspring. Hence, actions and their manifested consequences can be traced to generations past and future generations until such karma is 'cleared' or manifested in the form of response, effect...

Understanding

One might think that smiling at the cycles of life is a simple attitude or a state of mind — far from it. We smile when we are free from the past through our understanding of it, free from the past and its manifestations today, free from our past actions and their associated karma, today... Free because we understand, we understand that the manifestations today are conditioned by past actions... And it is this insight as to why an event is taking place (or understanding the outcomes of this event and how such outcomes have since affected our life) that makes us genuinely smile. As such, our resentment and resistance of today's manifestations and consequences stem merely from our lack of understanding, and are most likely the driving force behind our resentment.

Smiles ensue from freedom...
Smiles ensue from understanding the past...
Smiles ensue from making peace with the moment...
Smiles ensue from making peace with the past event itself
that might have caused us angst today...
Smiles ensue from making peace with the past...
Smiles ensue from making peace with the 'certainty' of our
future... the certainty of our finality on earth...

Hence, smiling at and understanding what happened and how our karma has affected, is affecting, and will continue to affect us, are synonymous in this case.

Nowadays, I smile as the event is taking place, as somehow, somewhere, this non-coincidence will be uncovered tomorrow or at some point in the future by my understanding, by the karmic path transcending the moment... As such, my smile today is leading me down the path of least resistance towards inner peace and transcendence, towards acceptance of the moment and a surrender to the unfolding of the karmic cycle, of the 'now' and its eventuality, of the 'future' and its manifestations.

The process of understanding might take many forms. One form could be the interlinking of past and current events with their outcomes in the now, the people that have since come into our lives, the changes in our state of mind because of them, and the ensuing inner growth we have experienced. Another form could be the renewed wisdom through which we see life and how accepting we are of certain people, actions, reactions, and/or life states. Yet another form could be the way in which we handle conflict, internal and external, and how we communicate within and with the world around us... Effectively, understanding is growth, is wisdom, and that is NO coincidence. Understanding is a conscious action to make the moment a state of peace, a state of karmic acceptance and clearance, a state of 'creative relativity'.

Creative Relativity

Creative Relativity is a state of consciousness, a state of awareness, a state of interlinking now with the past, with karma, with the events currently unfolding, with the potential unfolding of future events. We can reach an inner state of Creative Relativity all while preserving our freedom of interpretation, freedom of understanding, freedom of making sense of the manifestation of a karmic cycle, a cycle in life, our cycle in time...

Our cycle in time reflects our actions — be they conscious or subconscious, our karma, our learned and digested lessons, our reactions, our understandings, our pains and hurts, our conscience, our inner reflection and truth, our surrender to fate, to the power of this cycle... In time, our karmic cycle shall affirm the reality that all actions initiated in our cycle will become both actions and reactions in the future, reactions to the floating and circling good and ill wills, circling through our life, our time on this earth, and beyond.

With Creative Relativity, our cycle in time is directly linked to the people we are associated with in life, be they our partner or spouse, our children or parents, our extended family members or our friends, our work partners or our colleagues, etc. Inherent in such associations, by mere virtue of association, is the power to initiate actions on our cycle in time, our karmic cycle, our cycle in life, and effectively, bind their karmic cycles to ours such that we succumb to, and are submitted to, their actions and reactions over both our life and theirs. Accordingly, it is critical to be aware of our 'associates' in karmic cycles and their impact through our understanding of why events are taking place in our life as a result of such cycle binding.

Such awareness reveals a new dimension of understanding, one based on the inextricable relationship of cause and effect. The consequences of our actions today manifest themselves in our own lives and extend to the lives of our associates, partners, family members, society, and the nation. The presence of such a dimension inevitably leads to a state of no-coincidence as related to our life on earth and all those associated with us. The existence of a no-coincidence state rests on the notion of past actions and their future consequences. Hence, the awareness of and expectation of such consequences are critical to a deeper understanding and a conscious transcending of the individuals submitted to them.

Moreover, our karmic cycle may intertwine with the environment in which we live, hence, our need to carefully vote for the most suitable person in the position of effecting change and creating actions that bind a nation and bind us. The consequences of the actions of such elected individuals will affect the future of the environment we live in, and thus the karmic cycle of the nation. In the twentieth century, nowhere is the interconnectedness of the karmic cycle of individuals with the nation more evident than in Germany, Italy, and Russia through Adolf Hitler, Benito Mussolini, and Joseph Stalin, respectively. During the Second World War, their karmic cycles resulted in the deaths of tens of millions and ravaged the world. The consequences of their actions marked and affected the world for decades thereafter. Fair to say, the actions of Japan, the United States, France, the United Kingdom, and many other countries were as ravaging and widespread and caused economic and military hardship across the majority of nations.

Since the Second World War, the karmic cycles of the world have been caught up in the bipolarity of international relations between the United States and the Soviet Union for the good part of almost four decades, then between the United States and Russia. After which the world has been witness to the multipolarity of nations between the United States, the European Union, China, and Russia, with many more karmic cycles an almost certainty.

In summary, the Creative Relativity of how we create and receive karma, how we associate with the karmic cycles of others, be they family members, friends, associates, partners, neighbors, or national leaders, will be manifested depending on the extent to which we are affected by such Relativity cycles, by the way we approach life, deal with life, and impact our life and the lives of those people directly or indirectly linked to our karmic cycle. Such Creative Relativity, interwoven with past and present, affirms the lack of coincidences in life and the utmost need for all to be aware of the karmic cycles they are initiating now, in the moment, and their future ramifications.

There Are No Coincidences in Life...

When we are unaware of our Creative Relativity, and painful events manifest themselves in our life, we can easily choose to not understand, to react, to disregard the cycle of karma, our cycle in time, and, consequently, we easily shun the Creative Relativity cycle and pass the blame to a 'power' outside and beyond the self, to God's will, to an 'evil eye', to a 'curse' that someone somewhere inflicted and wished, to 'bad luck' that is tracking the self, and so on and so forth.

Such easy escape from the pain of understanding, from facing the self with accountability for actions past, actions and reactions riding our karmic cycle, is but a fleeting sensation, temporarily appeasing our inner pain, pushing our heads in the sand to ignore reality, ignore the manifestation of our karma as it rides our cycle in time... And when the self awakens from such a state of denial, denial that such events cannot be reduced to mere coincidences, only then can the self be free from the moment, free from the pain, and only then can the self actually smile in acceptance, in contentment, in freedom...

Words echo the spirit...
Actions echo values...

As such, when we talk, we relay how the spirit is affected by our values and our actions, and how we are intervening in this process of action, reaction, and the karmic cycle — all with Creative Relativity...

As we accept the state of Creative Relativity, consequences become a non-coincidence state — they become expected, or at least they lose the element of surprise, and our understanding of their very presence becomes much simpler, with the least resistance possible. Effectively, with the path of least resistance, we accept that such effects are not a coincidence and accept the fate bestowed upon us as a result of our karmic cycle, of our actions past, and of the actions of those karmic cycles bound to us.

Creative Relativity is manifested by the firm belief in a no-coincidence state in life, by the fact that there are no coincidences in the life we lead. Such a state is directly linked to our awareness of our actions, our karmic cycles, and our understanding of their manifestations around us.

Karma, I Am All Yours

What the future holds, what the future brings is beyond our control, and to this I smile as well. I doubt not that come what may tomorrow and the following day and every day thereafter, there is surely a lesson to be learned, an understanding to be unlocked, a deep meaning embedded within from which I will grow from and grow through.

Yes, there are NO coincidences in life, and with this belief, I am smiling, and I am serene...

Karma, I am all yours... Enjoy the Dance...

Art:

Of Creativity & Existentialism…

How deafening existential pain is… How easy it is for such pain to mute our mindfulness of life, our primordial energy of being… A suffering we endure just by being aware of our finality, our end as we *think* we know it…

Looking back in time at the different civilizations, cultures, and tribes confirms the omnipresence of such existential awareness through all the rituals associated with birth, marriage/union, and death. Our ancestors celebrated life through ceremonies of birth and union and showed respect for death and for the omni-powers of the spirits that reside in human beings through dance and fire rituals, exorcism of spirits, shamanism, prayer, and many other forms as documented over the ages on rocks, tombstones, mausoleums, manuscripts, etc…

Art

One form of existential awareness cuts across all such celebrations and rituals: art. Expressed uniquely within each culture and time period, the creative energy of art has been the key ingredient through such existential renderings of both the joys of life and the pains of death.

Over the ages, art manifested itself through paintings, drawings, sculptures, music, dance, theatre, humor, films, and numerous other forms that we know today. Such art forms have woven themselves into the societal fabric and its dance with life and through life. On some level, art manifestations have become part of our societal interactions, taken for granted without truly understanding the foundation of such creative human expression. It will be the arduous task of current and future generations to deeply digest the impetus of such art creations, to comprehend the drivers of its manifestations, its foundation in our subconscious self, and our awareness of it through the ages.

Creativity has enjoyed many unique forms and shapes through time and cultures. Moreover, independent of the uniqueness of form, art has been the answer to our existential questions. On a deeper level, the creative energy and expression of art numb our existential awareness, even if only for a fainting moment, and give us hope for tomorrow, hope that we 'are' still, we are 'here' long after we are gone.

In a nutshell, art creates continuums of expression. In other words, art inscribes the creator into the historic moment of creation, of rendering, of evaluation and re-evaluation, and of re-interpretation of such creation in the future. As such, art and creativity render the creator, in one way or another, immortal, with the potential of her/his art becoming part of the cultural expressions of generations to come, watching, listening to and interpreting this created art with the flair of the particular generation affected by it.

Art, with its many forms, and as we create it, helps us conquer existential pain, conquer death, conquer our longing for more time on earth.

Art renders our time on earth both indefinite and worthwhile, and pushes the boundaries of our existence on earth that much longer, that much wider...

On some level, art inscribes us, its creators, in eternity, enabling us to conquer the moment, conquer time, and transcend the now for many future rebirths through its creative powers, and its impact on both current and future generations...

Art and The War Child

As a war child myself, my existential pains, my fears of dying and of losing loved ones to the war machine, began to haunt me at a very young age. Such pains and fears have been lurking inside me, lodged in my subconscious mind, lodged in my inner being, appearing once in a while under the guise of protectionism, religious zeal, and other masks... What is real, though, is that I am a product of such extreme emotions and the transcendence of such fears comes, almost always, at a heavy price. Such a price is manifested through my nervous system, my inner unspoken fears, my fragility vis-à-vis loss.

Bearing such a load, a creative mind can't but erupt to release such pent-up anxieties, pent-up unanswered questions, pent-up anticipations of what is to come. And how powerful it is when the mind triumphs over fears. When I was ten years old, my first triumph was in the form of prayer, or the spiritual realm of life and the after-life — or so I wanted to believe.

Such a realm calmed my momentary fears of dying and helped me face death with a religious continuum. As war subsided, those fears became mixed with existential questions and pains and most questions remained unanswered, as religion no longer addressed the deeper questionings of life, existence, and beyond. The scientist in me was seeking far more tangible answers and the answers I found increased the existential pains and made them real in a supreme way. In my mid-twenties, extreme energies, induced by love and fleeting infatuations, fired in me the overwhelming urge to compose piano music. Such compositions, always improvised as I could not read nor write piano music, have been, to date, expressions of extreme energies, all imbued with my subliminal pains and joys and all life's affirmations.

As such, music, or my form of existential art, took center stage in my eternal expressions, my inscription in eternity, and continue to be one of my key transcendental dances with life, with death, with humanity, with my spirit…

Art and the Human Condition

When I look around me in Lebanon, and ponder the depth of the art produced over the past two centuries, in all fields and through many art forms, I can't but be in awe at the massive achievements and the breadth of the artists' reach, both locally and internationally.

As I dig deeper in the history of Lebanon, the history of wars and famines over the ages, and how such wars and famines accentuated the existential battles on a societal level and a personal level as individuals struggled for survival, what becomes apparent is how artistic expressions served as the oxygen for such pains, further heightening the power and universality of the artistic message. Without a doubt, the richness of the art created has been, and will continue to be, some of the best art Lebanon has produced to this day and for centuries to come.

One can expand on the above by contemplating the wars that ravaged Europe over the eighteenth and nineteenth centuries and analyzing the artistic masterpieces that ensued from such existential pains. Whether through operas, classical music, paintings and sculptures, and many other forms known then, I cannot but affirm that from the womb of those pains, such creative geniuses and mutated genes manifested themselves in beautiful and cross-generational art, art to alleviate the momentary pains, art to speak to us, to future generations, about its drivers and the state of the human condition back then, coded between its layers.

Art, effectively, transmits the human condition related to the existential pains at the time of its creation.

Expressed peacefully, in its own 'artistic' way, art transmits the full authenticity of the moments felt and the history of the lands affected by such pains.

Art documents memories…

Art echoes cultural and political movements within societies, nations, continents…

Art reflects the values of cultures…

Art distills the state of cultures and nations throughout history into the form that best reflects their character, their identity, their pain, their national experience, their karma…

For instance, one can easily see the impressionistic art of Claude Monet, Pierre-Auguste Renoir, Edouard Manet and many others reflecting the existential rendering of the spirit, or the faded memory of such moments in time, as we see non-defined silhouettes or the impression of those moments on canvas, and not the actual details of life, or the actual reflection of life as it was. Moreover, the cubistic art of Pablo Picasso, Georges Braque, and many others becomes the answer to the ravaging wars of the twentieth century, depicting bodies in a cubistic, mutilated way, representing both destroyed life and structures as a result of the destructive and mutilating world wars of 1914 and 1939. Additionally, the dramatic expressions of the classical music pieces composed during and post wars in Europe and the Middle East over the past three centuries reflect the fiery and emotional state at that time… Effectively, the music composed during the eighteenth, nineteenth, and twentieth centuries transcended the moments as screams against the predicament of societies when facing such uncontrollable fates. Such artistic forms are omnipresent in the music of Wolfgang Amadeus Mozart, Ludwig Van Beethoven, Richard Wagner, Giuseppe Verdi, Giacomo Puccini, Mohammad Abdel Wahab, Wadih Al Safi, Rahbani Brothers, and many others.

Art has become the echo, the reprimand, the documenter, the reporter, the film, the painting, the scream, the yell, the rebellion, all intertwined in the form that made the artist free to be and to express such existential pain across universal boundaries, without any formal resistance to such expression.

Over the ages, through its many forms, art has morphed into the authentic tool for documenting the history of nations... As we interpret such art and relate to it in the now, it is for us to judge how to hear it, view it, interact with it, and whether it echoes our current pains and addresses our current journeys...

Art...The Healer

Art is the echo inside the psyche of societies...

Art is a reflection of the human condition interacting within the sphere of humanity...

Art is the light within each paint brush...

Art is the silence between the operatic tones and notes...

Art is the grand stopper of time as we know it...

Art is the grand healer of societies from their eternal existential struggles with time and finality...

Faced with the certain finality of life, art is the answer to all the undocumented and unanswerable existential enquiries, more so now than during any times past.

For a short time, at least, art can be our guide to inner peace, to transcendence, to embracing the end as we know it, and yet cannot understand it.

For a short time, at least, art stops time to celebrate the creative energy lurking inside it, and frees our spirits to join the artist in the energy that made the art inscribed in the human subconscious mind, in the universality of creativity, in our temporary journey on earth.

I hereby kneel to you O Art, O Master, to your supreme and eternal power, and to all you have done and will do for our eternal journey, our eternal peace...

Impotence

Death and... Impotence

As an engineer, I have been trained in problem solving. However, 'life's' problems are a dimension requiring the utmost awareness, enlightenment, and inner peace... And no engineering background prepared me for what came and what is yet to come...

As such, the biggest problems I have faced in my life started with the self, with the psyche, with the subconscious self, with the unknown within, with the lurking demons within, with the unlearning of bad habits or thought processes, with the freeing of the spirit from all unnecessary loads, unnecessary guilt, unnecessary trappings — be they justified or not...

Many a problem have become unsolvable because we did not face them and diagnose them at the right time, early on. Many a problem have become non-tractable because the person or group or organization facing them did not accept their existence, did not declare their presence, did not seek assistance; rather they willfully misdiagnosed them and resumed as if all were well... Many a problem have become part of the status quo because we were afraid to face them, fix them, or end them.

At times, certain people in our lives become problematic, like a failed partnership, a failed marriage, a failed engagement of some sort, and we allow such failures to linger... The more we let them linger, the more we let the fear of separation, fear of failure, fear of our conscience pains, guilt, and the echoes of karma choke us... And the more we delay dealing with the problem, the more the problem becomes a sore we carry, a cross we lift every day in the hope it will go away, dissipate, become lighter, less painful to see, to bear, to deal with, to adapt to...

Essentially, at times, we become impotent in front of endings, not because we don't want to push such endings forward, but because we are afraid of them... Endings are hard, and, at times, unbearable with their ricochets on our life, the life of those in our karmic orbit, our conscious orbit, our inner peace, our cycle of life and in life...

Such impotence is only normal, as 'death' is an all-encompassing feeling in such cases. Our intuitive and subconscious reaction is to preserve life, preserve such engagements, while death is the opposite. Death requires sheer will, sheer *enough energy*, sheer transcendence and forgiveness of the self and the other person or institution with which such endings are sought...

Oh, how hard it is to face such decisions to end, and move on...

At times, endings are the only active decisions we make in order to move on...

At times, the abuse and molestations of such relationships are so immense to carry, immense for the spirit to make sense of, make light of, make peace with, that ending them is the only path forward…

We break our impotence to free our spirit, to free our inner self from the trappings of guilt, of our conscience, of the 'Christian' teachings of sacrifice, of the fear of death, of the fear of our own terminal state, our own death…

We can make peace with endings, with the wrong partner, with the wrong turn of events, with the wrong engagements, only when we make peace with death, our own death, the death of the future with such situations, such individuals, such institutions, such predicaments.

Organizations and… Impotence

If you have a problem I don't know about, you don't have a problem…

Problems are life tied up… And all that life needs in such cases is a bit of will to untie the problems, and get life back on track…

Problems are the spice of life, and more than ever, they enhance the meaning of life…

Facing and solving problems in life is an art. The art of accepting the existence of a problem, diagnosing the problem, analyzing the problem and its causes, creating solutions, testing solutions, and implementing solutions…

After all, problems are a sign of health in organizations, a sign that the organization is alive, growing, learning… Granted some problems can be terminal for organizations, but early handling of and dealing with any problem are key to reducing the gravity of their impact on the affected organization. In essence, problems are a sign that something is wrong, a sign that something that was once working has chocked up a bit and needs some assistance to start working again. Problems may also be an indicator that a process requires some assistance to go live, to launch…

Creative solutions to 'problems' are what made the industrial, transportation, computer, online, and artificial intelligence revolutions a reality, with many more to come.

When we address the core of why problems become cancers in organizations, of why certain problems rendered such organizations impotent to face and solve them, we can most certainly trace such impotence to 'communication' — be it the absence of communication, the ineffectiveness of communication, both across and within organizational levels, or harmful communication in the form of intimidation and bullying… In most cases, such communication problems are manifested through the insecurity and reluctance of managers to share problems, to communicate them, to acknowledge them, to simply solve them and move on…

Silence and… The Ostrich Syndrome

One of the worst styles of communication, and effectively the worst enemy of organizations facing problems, is 'silence': the act of passive communication or, more precisely, the act of non-communication, the act of hiding the problem verbally and not sharing it with the organization's governing body, the act of saying nothing, and, to a certain extent, the act of pretending a problem does not exist, i.e. 'the ostrich syndrome'… Many a time such 'silence' camouflages the problem, all while the problem remains undetected by the 'body' of the organization, all while it grows in seriousness, in size, in non-tractability, affecting other divisions within the organization, metastasizing to various divisions, and silently becoming the cancer that no one consciously wants to acknowledge, the elephant in the room that no one is willing to see or deal with...

Fear of breaking the silence can prove to be quite overwhelming for a perfectionist leader, effectively rendering her/him impotent vis-à-vis such a management problem.

A leader afraid of failure, afraid to acknowledge, afraid of the impact of breaking such silence, of letting the truth out, of communicating the problem and freeing it to become the organization's problem for all to chip in and solve, is a non-existent leader, a non-effective leader, an impotent leader...

The Ostrich Syndrome is prevalent and can be traced to the leader's individualistic approach to problem solving, and, at times, to a cultural syndrome in diagnosing and communicating problems. The cultural syndrome is very dangerous and can lead to massive failures interlocked with both the persona and the impotence of the leader, all because the culture's reverence to the leader transcends any wrongdoing and makes of the silence the modus operandi of the moment, until the leader decides otherwise.

Silence — Case in Point

South Korea's Aviation Industry has suffered many deadly crashes, the majority of which were due to the national cultural syndrome of preserving hierarchy, asking few questions of leaders, one-way/top-down communication, and almost non-existent bottom-up communication. When the co-pilots were reserved about alerting the leader of problems, assuming the pilots were aware of and silent about them, the result was numerous crashes over the past decades. Almost all such crashes were attributed to a broken form of communication between pilots and co-pilots, a communicative style deeply rooted in cultural traditions and modalities of relating to senior leaders and elders.

Silence and Counter-Silence

"When no one is to blame...
Everyone is to blame."
Pope Francis on the indifference to
Human suffering around the world.

Nevertheless, both executives and staff within each organization need to develop a kind of vigilance for this deadly silence, the 'silent killer', resulting from such a syndrome... And the simplest of forms is to acknowledge the problem and ensuing silence, and develop a healthy style of communication, a healthy challenge, a healthy cause and effect rapport within, as related to problems and their repercussions on the organization, their positive impact on learning, on growing, on the common experience gained within... Choosing to deal with a problem can be a group effort in order to break the silence, break the impotence, and preserve the health of the organization across its many layers of management.

Incompetence and... Impotence

More often than not, in family-built organizations, the incompetence of family leaders and/or managers in dealing with problems is easily masked by their impotence in solving a problem, or their silence related to a problem they participated in causing. Sometimes, locked into a self-image, a self-inflated persona, the ma/patriarch of a family-built organization will resort to all kinds of tools and techniques to mask a problem, 'shove it under the rug', hide it, stay silent about it, hoping the problem would somehow go away unnoticed... To the point where, in certain family organizations, the ma/patriarch resorts to firing any employee who breaks the silence in a desperate attempt to hide the intricacies of such a problem, its causes, and its ensuing losses and impact on the organization... Effectively, s/he wanted to hide its impact on her/his image, ego, concocted persona, and, ultimately, hide from facing the death of the phenom s/he built in her/his eyes and the eyes of the family...

Solving a problem can easily be handled, by hiring a capable professional with the necessary experience, after it gets diagnosed and acknowledged. However, incompetence is another face of impotence, and when impotence and hesitation become intertwined with incompetence, the problem becomes that much harder to solve as the ego of the leader and/or manager becomes a player in the solution and can easily hinder the development of the solution. Effectively, ego, the nucleus of incompetence, makes of the leader/manager the problem, the cancer, and the only way to solve this problem is by removing such a leader from the position s/he is in. When the leader is the ma/patriarch, a key founder, a key family member, or the chairman of the board of directors of the organization, removing such a leader becomes a suicidal note for the internal dynamics of the organization or the family-built institution, and can cause severe communication and financing failures in retribution for such firing/removal. In such cases, the death of the ego of the leader becomes the hara-kiri note that the problem solver has to recommend to the board or leadership of the organization, and a series of deep discussions need to follow in order to reach a peaceful conclusion.

At a subtler level, such manifestation of impotence could have its roots in the leader's psyche, inner learning, lack of inner reflections and self-awareness as related to the intricacies of such leadership situations, and how to deal with problems, with death — her/his own death or the organization's death... On some level, dealing with such dimensional dysfunction, both leader and organization need to learn how to deal with incompetence, with non-clarity, with non-conformity, with non-essence, with transparency, with vulnerability...

At its core, when the leader is the problem, and the leader is resisting such acknowledgement, it is, again, the leader's fear of, and struggle with, death that is at play and at the root of such manifestations. Effectually, it is the death of her/his role in the organization, the death of her/his meaning, the death of her/his dream, the death of time, her/his own death...

Notably, all the above fears and death-forms that a leader has to deal with and transcend are existential energies that the leader needs to make peace with before accepting the role of the leader, before accepting the problem at hand, before accepting the ensuing recommended solutions... And such acceptance attempts are very hard to practice, let alone live through...

Manifestations of Mental Impotence

With mental impotence, the leader or manager becomes overwhelmed with insecurity and unable to face the problem at hand. As such, fear takes over, and with fear, hesitation sets in, and with hesitation, the worst nightmares and fears surface. Such fears render the leader paralyzed, unable to move…

"Let me assert my firm belief that the only thing we have to fear is… fear itself — nameless, unreasoning, unjustified terror which paralyzes needed efforts to convert retreat into advance." Franklin D. Roosevelt

Mentally impotent individuals can easily be spotted with certain characteristic behaviors. Such individuals, females or males, usually resort to:

- Intimidation
- Bullying
- Yelling, raising their voice, especially in front of crowds
- Unstable gesturing
- Character assassination of colleagues, partners, or subordinates
- Verbal abuse
- Excessive honesty to mask their disingenuous spirit
- Poisoning the environment with vile words and behavior
- Viciousness in tackling problems
- Abuse of knowledge and divulging other individual's confidential information to advance a certain agenda
- Distrust of others, masking their distrust in themselves
- Engaging as solo players to hide their impotence
- Transforming themselves into fake artists: fake emotions, fake spirit, fake demeanor, fake energy, fake everything…

As such, mentally impotent individuals are mentally unstable and can resort to many forms of abuse to mask such impotence, even to physical violence... The core of this impotence is displayed with their behavior around strong personalities, partners or associates, individuals that awaken the impotence within them... In certain cases, mental impotence manifests itself with the denial of the individual's lack of ability, with a deep rooted energy of jealousy, with cowardly maneuvers, with coveting what other individuals have without the appreciation of their own abilities, gifts, and strengths... Individuals with such traits will continuously struggle with internal demons, foggy wisdom, inferiority complexes, unstable reactions, all ingrained within a profoundly weak character...

The above manifestations bode ill for any organization whose leader embodies such forms of behavior and can result in the resignation of its top executives, or for partnerships to crumble, or for family businesses to split... In short, such non-addressed manifestations can be cause for non-communication, for the 'death silence', for cancers to develop within organizations, for a total loss of value.

Again, this vicious cycle of impotence can only be broken by communicating, seeking help, admitting the existence of a problem, and resolving its manifestation with full transparency, honesty, compassion, sacrifice — even if it means sacrificing the leader to save the organization... Even if it means the 'death' of the leader...

Sex and... Impotence

In the common vernacular, the most prevalent use of the word impotence is related to male erectile dysfunction, and the associated sexual impairment, sexual stress on couples, risk of divorce, potential violent eruptions by the male, and so on...

Sexual impotence can be treated with specific medications for most cases. Some cases are mostly psychological, and as such, their treatment is far subtler and requires a different approach, including communication between the couple, and seeking the aid of a therapist.

In relationships, sexual impotence can lead to existential struggles, all while facing the potential of separation, of divorce, of the death of the relationship, the death of the sexual desire of the partner, and numerous other intricate dimensions.

Such struggles are deep, complex, and have dimensions related to each person suffering from such a predicament. At the core, sexual impotence represents the death, in one way or another, of either sexual desire, sexual function, relationship status, self-image of a male, and much more. Such struggles are not simple, but manageable, once the ending is accepted, and the death-form is dealt with and treated for what it is. Being transparent with all the emotions that accompany this struggle is key for the healing process to reach a true and honest state for all involved.

Again, accepting, communicating, transcending are pathways to treating any form of impotence, be it sexual or mental. All it takes is the freeing of the taboo associated with either, and impotence is on its way to being resolved, healed, and surpassed.

Life and... Impotence

We are all born impotent... and will die impotent...
We are all impotent in front of death, our predicament...
We are all impotent with our inability to stop or slow down
the death march...

Human beings have tried forever and a day to stop the death clock or, better yet, delay it… Our ancestors have created concoctions to preserve life, to extend life… The pharmaceutical and medical industries are reaping billions of dollars from the fear of death, from the willingness of individuals to pay all amounts of money to extend life, to win some time against death, to conquer the giant sounds and pains of the human impotence vis-à-vis the end… and how sad and lonely this fight is, as, to date, there have been no winners… And there never will be…

On some level, men are more prone to experience impotence than women, as women have the ability to 'give life', to carry life in their wombs, to procreate, and as such, permeate life and conquer death through procreation, albeit temporarily. Such power in women makes of their impotence regarding death somewhat less omnipresent than it is with men, but nevertheless, present.

In the end, death will win… sadly…

Impotence is the most celebrated trait of human beings on earth…

All living humans will have the 'joy and honor' of going through some form of death ritual, where death will celebrate such rooted impotence in front of the world, having the last laugh, dancing on our graves, sarcastically, mockingly, sadistically, sardonically, and without any remorse, regret, or sorrow…

O Death… Until our eternal encounter, I am the one laughing now… And for a while, I hope…

44

Have You?

Have You Heard the Earth Breathe?
Have You Watched the Sea Sleep?
Have You Witnessed the Sky Cry?
Have You Listened to the Sun Whisper?

Have You Hugged a Mountain?
Have You Run with a Cloud?
Have You Heard the Silence of Time?
Have You Recovered from the Kiss?

Have You Embraced Your Addiction to Oxygen?
Have You Met Eternity?
Have You Forgiven Death?
Have You Awakened?

Have You?

The Ethics of Silence

Knowledge is power…
Truth is supreme…
Honor is life…
Dignity is existence…

The Ethics of Silence is when we are silent about truth in order to honor the dignity of a human being, a family, a society, a nation, protect their spirit, and assist their will to be, to survive, to fight.

The Ethics of Silence is when we do not mention the truth, and even lie, temporarily, in order to protect the spirit of the person affected by the 'truth', by the 'information', by the 'facts', and, consequently, slow the impact of such truth on their being, in the hope of assisting such person, such spirit, absorb such facts when their spirit is ready, if ever…

The truth lives inside us. We all know what is true, within our own frame of reference. We all have a compass of what is right and what is wrong. We all honor the truth, deep within. Sometimes, for ethical and/or emotional reasons, we choose to ignore the calling of truth, the inner voice of this compass, the inner voice of conscience and reason, the inner voice of dignity and honor… However, we soon realize that truth is not a choice but a fact. And as such, masking it will make of truth a solid force in the face of who we are, in the face of our dignity, our honor.

When such truth can cause harm to certain individuals, to families, to communities, to nations, and limit their spirit, hinder their progression and evolution towards their goals, the ethics of silencing such truth becomes evident, omnipresent, as the price of truth is much higher than the price of such ethical silence at the moment, in the now… Sometimes, certain truths are freeing when shared, but this sense of freedom may come at the expense of family unity, societal bonds, or it may be more costly with the price being our own inner peace.

The knowledge of truth is always a double-edged sword. We can choose to deploy it, or stay silent about it, but doing nothing is not a choice. Staying silent about the truth is as much a choice as sharing the truth. It is our right and duty to choose which action, *at the right time*. Active ethical silence is making of truth an important tool to deploy at the right time. As such, freeing the truth within from the bounds of right and wrong and making use of it to impact both the people and the situation at hand, is our choice to make, in the moment, when the time is right.

The right time to break the silence is as important as the silence about any fact one knows…

Knowledge and truth are important, but more important is how and when we deploy them.

When the right time to release the truth comes, the ethics of any silence frees all interlinked facts out in the open, frees the hearts and minds to understand and transcend…

The Ethics of Silence and My Father: The Final Journey…

In February of 1994, my father was diagnosed with pancreatic cancer and flown to Houston for treatment. After thorough CAT scans, the doctors confirmed that my father's cancer had metastasized to his liver, reducing his cancer survival period to a few months, if not weeks.

When we discovered this 'truth' about my father's condition, knowing that my father would not fight should he know that the cancer had metastasized, the whole family and I chose to stay ethically silent about the liver metastasis. Rather, we focused our energy and efforts on helping my father fight the cancer with all the will he had… and we had.

The Ethics of Silence is love expressed silently, discreetly…

With the knowledge of such facts, my whole system was in shock; my stomach was cramping, my digestive system was overstressed and blocked, and severe liver pains set in — all symptoms of anxiety and stress, and yet, omnipresent in the way I was facing such truth, and the ethics of my silence associated with it. I wanted to talk about my pain and my father's predicament to the world in the hope of alleviating my anxieties, but unfortunately, I could not and would not. My silence made me feel worse inside, but that was my choice then, and I lived with such a choice, and never regretted it.

I loved my father dearly. I choked up whenever I was around him. I so artfully masked all my fears, my anger, my all-encompassing helplessness… I cried alone. I wrote about my anxieties and anger deep into the nights; when all had succumbed to slumber, my fingers would paint my thoughts, my madness, my impotence, my screams, my tears, my pains, all while the deafening silence of death was approaching… And every morning, I would wake up ready for the fight, ethically silent about the truth, masking my fears and anxieties with love and care, and lying oh so masterfully for six months to my father's face, all while knowing I would lose the fight, all while knowing he would die and I would lose the sight of him… Oh how hard it was to stay ethically silent, to lie, to pretend, to hide from him what I knew, and yet, in the face of such hardships day in and day out, I fought as if we were going to win, and he would survive…

Yes, I struggled with my ethical silence… It was so hard to say the truth, and so hard to keep it in… I was struggling with accepting his death, struggling with accepting my own death… I was struggling continuously with my fear of loss, and my fear of pain stemming from such a grand loss in my life on my consciousness…

I was struggling continuously with whether I should tell him the truth or stay silent… I thought a lot about sharing the gravity of his illness with him, but could not proceed… I was constantly struggling with the guilt I would feel should his health take a sudden turn for the worst… And the cycle went on and on, without any recourse to the 'truth' during the whole period… It was as if I had mastered the art of lying, albeit for a noble cause, and yet, remained composed in front of the finality, without any hope of coming out winners on the other end of the tunnel…

When I asked my father if he wanted to do another cycle

of chemotherapy, he replied: "Son, if we have a five per cent chance to survive, go for it... just do it" ... And we would go for it just to keep hope, keep the fight, pump up his morale. Meanwhile, the ethics of my silence was killing me inside, tearing me apart, making me scream inside, without him to share my pain with... He was my pillar of strength and watching him fizzle into the illness' ravaging cycles made me feel so impotent, so scared, so helpless in front of the predicament, his death...

On August 18, 1994, my father died... Painfully, I never violated the ethics of my silence...

12

One day, my twelve-year-old son and I were walking together inside a shopping mall. All of a sudden, my son asks for permission to leave my side and roam the mall alone, without me guarding him, free from my presence, my shadow... Simply, free. He wanted to discover, to look for something he wanted to buy, alone, in freedom. Perhaps he just wanted to feel that he could do that without me being with him, near him, without me being there to guide him, protect him... or better yet, protect me from my fears over him...

For a moment I cringed, and then I said yes.

My son left me before we agreed when and where we would meet again; without a cell phone, I had no way of calling him...

When he left my side to wander alone, discover alone, I stood still, in silence, in my aloneness, in my fears, in my rejection, in my existential inner screams, wanting my son's progression into adulthood to slow down, wanting his childhood dependency to not end this abruptly, to last a bit longer, to be more merciful on my spirit, on my soul, on my own awareness of aging...

I searched for him, from afar, and found him, twice...

Each time my eyes would fall upon him, my anxieties would settle, I would choke up, and my eyes would well up with tears, tears of joy, of fear, of possessiveness, of selfishness, of not letting go, of not wanting to let go, of resistance, of inner pain, of pain with my own growth as a father, as a parent...

On some level, I knew I was resisting the inevitable goodbye that will happen one day, I just never expected to feel it so soon, when my son was just a twelve-year-old boy... He was growing into a man, and that pleased and pained me at the same time.

Somehow, I was afraid of letting me go, letting me accept my leaving, my end, my finality, the finality of my time on earth, with him, around him... I was afraid of letting go of a meaning of mine, my son growing into his own, growing to become independent of me, and growing up to be...

What an existential cry this reminder was... A harsh wake-up call it was... A harsh pain for where I was going, and how I was heading towards death, slowly, ignoring it, pretending it did not exist, forgetting its knocks on my spirit...

Oh well, I tried to resist that day. I cried. I resisted some more, but after a while, I pretended to accept it, and started looking for books at a nearby bookstore... Pretending is an understatement, but nevertheless, real... I was pretending to forget my separation anxieties, pretending to transcend my growing old pains, pretending that I was fine... Or so I made it look so on the outside...

After an hour or so, he joins me again, finished with his rounds for new games and toys, his discovery, his journey alone, his journey without me around, his journey within...

That day, we returned home as two adults with all the pride and joy in our hearts, and all the pains and cries in mine casual get-togethers, true but not conflicted conversations, peaceful encounters planned ahead and without high expectations — all with a controlled frequency per encounter and type of encounter. A high frequency will force the encroachment on privacy, as the usual, typical, surface-level, non-invasive topics would have been covered, and the conversations will delve into the personal, and hence, break the smart middle, and its benefits in maintaining the light nature of the friendship.

Smart Middle: The Art

Finding the smart middle is an art as it is unique for every person, family member, or friend. More importantly, the smart middle is an attitude towards relationships in general. We have to constantly be aware of where the boundaries of this middle are, and when they are crossed. Through laziness and manipulations, very frequent encounters, unawareness and vulnerability, the smart middle can easily be crossed by close family members and/or friends without our conscious consent, and without our awareness at times. Such crossing can be due to the absence of meaning in the life of the friend or family member. Such lack of meaning can erase such smart middle, push such a relationship into our realm of privacy, and steal our meaning, our inner peace, our inner calm, just because it makes the other party feel better.

As such, the smart middle is where we stay vigilant about our inner calm, inner sanctum, and protect our meaning and our friendships, without resorting to pushing them away or ridding ourselves of them.

Such vigilance comes from awareness, from the fact that we cannot rid ourselves of family, and from the fact that we

for accepting the end of boyhood in my son, for accepting the eternal goodbyes…

I have never forgotten how I felt that day, and probably never will.

To My Son

I bid you peace my boy, my son… I love you more than you could fathom and ask you to forgive me if I ever treated you with my own selfishness, treated you brutally with my own existential struggle, treated you with my rejection of my end, my end around you, my end in your life…

Please forgive this old and weak man who is your father, struggling to let you go, struggling to let himself go, to exit…

I bid me peace my son, because I am going to need it, badly… and sadly…

The Smart Middle

Many times in life, we allow ourselves to get close to certain individuals. But too much closeness always comes at a price: expectations increase drastically, communication becomes too personal, interventions in each other's lives become the norm, and the privacy of each person becomes optional.

And such relationships probably started as simple acquaintances, simple friendships, simple get-togethers. Why we allow such relationships to get too close is always a personal choice, a decision we make, a premeditated act that we pursue. In the midst and in the depth of such an interaction, taking a step back becomes difficult and might lead to separation conflicts, blame games, manipulations — be they emotional or mental… Simply put, bringing such closeness back to a balanced state of friendship is no easy task, it makes the engagements forward too difficult and may lead to a violent rupture of this close friendship that has pushed the boundaries of a healthy human connection…

Mind you, such violent ruptures are not simple to manage, can be hard to swallow, and will most probably cause deep internal conflicts and guilt trips with oneself: "Did I do the right thing? Why did I let it reach this level? Why wasn't I

more tolerant?" Moreover, such ruptures ca[n] games with one's partner where the expectatio[n] preventing us from being in such a predican[ment] place is exposed, revealed… It's much simpl[e] own actions, actions that led to this 'too clo[se] rather than justify them in terms of our own i[n] smart and healthy middle… And last, after se[paration], separation, the rupture gives us a sense of fr[eedom] load this relationship was, and allows us to b[e] all because we allowed the interactions to get t[oo] own comfort and the relationship to become a [burden to] carry rather than an enriching encounter to see[k].

Smart Middle: Find It

The obvious people to get too close t[o are our] siblings, friends, children, business partn[ers,] colleagues, parents of our childr[en,] prayer/yoga/sports partners, and the list g[oes on. The] problem with all the above is that we canno[t have a] clean-cut separation from such individuals if w[e want, or] if we do not respect the smart middle between u[s. Setting] limits on such relationships becomes too difficu[lt with the] many kinds of expectations and manipulations [they] can pressure the other one into.

Friends are great for our wellbeing, and f[orm for] us a solid support infrastructure that we have to [cherish. But] to avoid such conflicts and potential ruptur[es, we must] respect the smart middle. The smart middle i[s being] close enough, but not too close, and far enough[.] The smart middle is where we limit our clos[eness,] interventions, unassuming questions, simp[le]

need friends in our lives…

Hence, with such totalities and basic truths, the smart middle is a must to respect and to fight for in order to maintain peace in those relationships. The smart middle becomes a balancing act between our needs and the needs of the relationship to be sustained, with all the closeness required for such relationship to remain real, authentic, and honest.

After all, we need our friends, our family, and they need us. It is our duty to protect such sweet and real relationships from becoming toxic, and be able to sustain their oxygen for us to collaborate in making our journey in life easy, fun, fulfilling, entertaining, and real.

To all my friends and family members, thank you for the moments…

Death... My Friend

The Death March

Death started in my life as an enigma...

As a child, I always associated death with the marching music played by the 'death' band following the coffin, accompanied by the cries, screams, and the wails of praise to the deceased. The family members walk behind the coffin, holding hands, red-eyed, and emotionally distraught. It was ceremonial of some sort, even though the music had a very somber effect on me, with all the brass and drumming instruments 'firing at all cylinders' while marching toward the grave to perform the Christian burial rituals. The coffin would always pass in front of our house in Kab-Elias, Bekaa Valley, Lebanon. Sometimes, the coffin would be open, and we could see the dead person inside... The sight, as displeasing as it was, spiked my curiosity many times, tempting me to go and watch the burial procedure.

I was scared to accompany the crowd towards the graveyard, the Moozayyaneh (the Decorated) as we called it. Nevertheless, one day, at the age of seven, I mustered the strength and followed them...

The roads were empty and all stores closed their doors

momentarily as the coffin passed, as tradition dictated... The sound of the closing and opening of the doors still chimes in my head, as if the dead person had been watching and expecting such an act...

People would take turns in carrying the coffin, and, as a child, I was always worried they would drop it. The coffin was heavy and made of solid wood, the color of which varied from dark brown to white, depending on the age of the deceased — white was usually reserved for the young ones... As if the dead in the graveyard would notice the difference and prepare an exceptional welcome... As if the dead person in the coffin would notice the difference and the white colored coffin would appease her/his pain of an early exit... As if the color is a heads-up for Jesus during the resurrection that this dead person died young... Many more 'as ifs', but a loss is still a loss, early or late, and it's just as hard on the close family members and close friends 'left behind'... Left behind, although commonly expressed in this context, is somewhat inaccurate as all will follow, for sure, the same path, the same ritual, the same rite of passage through this solemn and omnipresent death march.

Part of the crowd following the coffin was the priest of the congregation to which the dead person belonged.

The priest would be praying along the way, all while the band would be firing those horns without slowing down, as if their actions were asking, pleading for the dead person's spirit to return, a resurrection of sort, but surreal, nevertheless.

When both crowd and coffin reached the graveyard, the death band music would stop, the priest would open the main gate, and a relative of the deceased would open the gate of the private family mausoleum. Such a sight was somber, to say the least... It was traumatizing for me, a seven-year-old boy, watching this for the first time.

The Mausoleum

The one fear that came over me when I was watching the mausoleum door open was: what if the person in the coffin were not dead and would wake up only to find her/himself inside this dark and closed room? What if s/he would die from fear inside this room with other dead bodies, banging at the mausoleum door with no one to listen, to hear, to help...? The 'what ifs' racing through my head and all these unanswered questions left hanging in my imagination, increased my anxieties of what was happening exponentially...

Watching the priest perform the final prayer ritual before the mausoleum door was closed was very emotionally charged with all the final words and final goodbyes and endless tears, all the flowers laid to adorn the burial site as if to celebrate this passing with the beautiful distinct scent of white roses and carnations...

The flowers were packaged either in a large circular-shaped arrangement, or a large cross-shaped one, with a white ribbon across each and words of praise from family members and/or friends to the person to be buried. The arrangements were left at the gate of the burial mausoleum, as if to decorate this sinister place of eternal silence, of meditation!

What an intense ritual this was to watch for the first time... I returned home, pale faced, scared, feeling nauseous, and full of anxieties that I could neither understand nor fathom. Such fears were all-encompassing and took hold of me for several days... The sight of the coffin being pushed inside the mausoleum, and the priest performing the final prayer rituals with his dark black robe, black beard, and long black hat, were all ingrained in my memory with all the anxieties stemming from the 'what ifs' still racing in my mind, without any sign of slowing down...

My mum gave me special water in the 'fear cup' or 'tasset al ra3be' as we called it, and my aunt caressed both my face and my back as she said a prayer to alleviate my fears and rid me of the 'evil spirit'... or was it the 'death spirit'?... Who knew?

Oh, how surreal those moments were, and still are when I remember them now, recollect their sights and sounds, with all the nostalgia of the moment, but not the event itself...

1970

My journey with death anxieties and discovery started early, way before the graveyard visit. With an anomaly in my cardia, where my stomach valves would not close well, I lost a lot of weight the first few months after I was born because I could not hold food down, to the point where my mother would help me go to sleep standing up for more than six months, well wrapped in my newborn cloth, all in order for me to digest the food I was eating... All in order to 'survive'.

I am sure my subconscious self was fighting such bouts of friendship with death from a very early stage in my life... From the day I was born, I guess... And such is the predicament of every human being on earth... So much I know, now...

The cardia anomaly manifested itself all throughout my life. As a child, liquid foods, mixed with acids from the stomach, would travel up my esophagus, and burn my throat, my tonsils, and induce chronic infections. I can still remember taking so many antibiotics when I was a child, all related to infections of the tonsils. The infections were so frequent that my pediatrician recommended my tonsils be taken out... Instead of fixing the cause, the doctor removed the symptom... Oh well, so much for medicine and its impact on our lives...

Many a time, medical doctors arrange either brief encounters and/or eternal journeys of their patients with death... As human beings, doctors have erred and will err, to the joy and merciless smiles of death, the ever-present death, waiting, rejoicing, and ready to pounce... I suppose death has friends and agents on earth, as much as miracle makers and life givers have... It all depends on how experienced these doctors are, and the depths of their conscience — all death antidotes, for a while at least...

Taking out the tonsils involved a full-fledged operation, with hospital entry, anesthesia, needles, serum, anxiety, the works... When I was admitted to the hospital, I was accompanied by both my mother and her eldest sister. My aunt did not have any children and I always treated her as my second mother, with all the sweetness and serenity of such a relationship with this grand woman. The night before the operation, with my mother and aunt sleeping in the same room with me at the hospital, I sat in bed, crying, scared of dying, scared of the unknown, scared of this first operation, and what it entailed... As a five-year-old boy, I started praying that all would go well, and I would be back home safely, safe with my family, my friends, my Matchbox cars... Safe from death... So much for what I knew then, what I did not know, and probably will never know — I guess...

I could not wait until the break of dawn and I started sharing my night 'events' with my mother and aunt. As the operation timing got closer, my hands got colder and my fear escalated. The hospital nurses came in the room to prepare me and took me to nowhere I was familiar with. I asked for my father, and luckily, he was right there, near me, holding my hand before I went into the operating room. I did not want to let go of his hand, but he kissed me, did the sign of the cross on my forehead, and I went in...

Inside the operating room, it was cold, and the doctor was trying to humor me, while the nurses were getting me ready... After a few seconds, I was totally knocked out by the anesthetic. I don't remember anything post, except the grogginess and the throat pain when I woke up in my room, on my bed... I was having a very hard time swallowing and kept on asking whether the operation went well... During those first few hours post-op, I forgot the fear I had felt going in because I was dealing with my immediate pain — my throat pain, and in doing so, I transcended my anxieties, my nightmare, the 'fear of death' journey...

1975

On April 10, 1975, my uncle died. I was ten. I remember that the whole Notre Dame des Apotres School in Kab-Elias knew about his passing. One of my friends came from lunch at his house near the school and told me how he died at the town doctor's clinic from a heart attack. My mother's eldest brother had passed away at forty-eight years of age.

I found out at noon, during school recess. I remember my stomach cramping at the news, my intestines totally locked, and a nauseous feeling overwhelmed me inside. At three p.m., just as I was getting ready to go back home in the school bus, the whole sky was loaded with dark clouds and it started to rain.

Looking at the clouds then, I distinctly felt as if nature

were weeping for my uncle's passing. I felt the rain on my face, as if nature's tears were sharing my pain of this first and major passing in my life...

My grandmother was in the hospital then, and could not assist with the burial preparations of her eldest. The family made sure never to tell her about his passing. However, she asked for him, and she asked and asked, and never got a straight answer — somewhere, somehow, she knew he had passed, but was too afraid to admit it within.

During the burial, as usual, the coffin passed in front of our house... This time, it was an open coffin. I watched my uncle's body from the balcony through teary eyes.

From their balconies, people were throwing rice and candy on the coffin... I am sure this ritual has its roots in the mythology of death, after death, the body transformation, and the spirit passing, but all I could see then was an expression of sorrow and pain by those who knew him and loved him, and were sad that he had passed so soon in life, and threw rice and candy violently at the coffin as an expression of deep sorrow.

The music from the brass instruments sounded differently that day... I heard the drums with every heartbeat, every stick, every strike... I kept feeling the music screaming at him to wake up, to get up, refusing to let him go...

That was the first death march I witnessed where I could not go and did not want to go to the graveyard. My father was marching with them, I saw him from the balcony, I wanted to wave but could not... To this day, I cannot forget my mother's face looking outside the window that day, crying, not communicating, not saying a word to express her pain, just gazing silently outside, with tears running down her face...

Death snatched one of us this time... Too close for

'comfort'... Many a nightmare ensued... Many a question went unanswered... What if death snatched my father? My mother...? I had trouble sleeping for many nights, as if guarding my parents from death, guarding my spirit...

War

In 1975, three days after my uncle's death, the civil war erupted in Lebanon. The cramping in my stomach increased and my fear of death became omnipresent... The state of war was all encompassing.

I was trained to kill in 1975, at the age of ten, trained to arrange meetings between villains and God, trained to dance with death, trained to protect my family, as one of the family 'adults', supposedly. I carried machine guns and grenades during those early years of war. I learned to befriend death, and learned to observe death approaching, ever so silently...

My father survived two car-bombing assassination attempts during the war, one in 1976 and the other in 1978.

One fateful day in 1976, the whole family escaped certain death from the more than sixty bombs that hit our homes and the Arak Touma manufacturing plant in Kab-Elias. With grenades and machine guns by my side, with bombs falling all around us during that day, the only sanity savior for me was a prayer booklet that my grandmother had given me. Kneeling on the floor, leaning against a barrel of alcohol inside the Arak Touma manufacturing plant, surrounded by the Touma mothers and family children, some crying while others eating or sleeping, I prayed all through the night of that sad and memorable day. After the bombing calmed down, my father and uncles cleared the way for the family members to leave the plant's basement and head towards my grandmother's home. At four a.m., we left the plant with sights of the village burning, and the sunlight barely starting to break over the mountain.

Holding on to my prayer booklet, in my war outfit, I slept on the sofa at my grandmother's house for a few hours, not knowing whether I would wake up…

I still remember how scared I was before leaving my grandmother's house that day, how scared I was while standing in front of the family house, watching the guards carry the young kids down to the manufacturing plant's lower floor, how scared I was while going down post… Simply, I did not know what to expect…

More importantly, after that night of continuous bombing, of crying, of screaming, and of my intense prayers, I remember I was never scared of death again… It was as if something in me accepted death, accepted the finality, accepted that there is a higher meaning to life, accepted that the journey begins whenever we make peace with death, accepted the terminal nature of death… It was as if I befriended death and death started to be a constant in my life, a 'loyal companion' of some sort… or so I thought…

I faced many death threats during the war. I was shot at several times, stabbed, beaten, and yet, I cannot but see myself as a war child, a war survivor, a warrior who is ready to stop another similar war in Lebanon, at any cost…

I know war is a death feast, but I am hoping that death will understand my position as a friend, and accept it… Maybe not… Oh well…

Aloneness

In 1983, at the age of eighteen, I had to leave Lebanon due to the ravaging war and associated risks… Commuting to a university in Beirut was very dangerous and continuing my studies was a must at the time... I still remember how surreal the goodbyes were at home and at the airport... I was so emotional, and yet full of hope to explore the new dimension that I was embarking on... It was my first time travelling to the United States, and my first time leaving home, under such conditions...

Soon after I arrived, my maternal grandmother died... It was very hard to deal with such a loss, and my mother could not attend the funeral due to war related road closures. Far away, her passing was a warning call of how fragile 'life' back home was, my family, my friends... And probably still is.

The silence of death approaching is very deceiving and unconventional...

Death, the hunter, is always on the prowl, ready to pounce on the next victim, without any mercy, or concept of wait...

Overwhelmed with physical pain and suffering, the human spirit calls upon death to free it from the body it is in, and the cycle goes on...

We are never ready to receive death peacefully...

Death always comes with a sense of sourness, deception, selfishness, carelessness...

Death comes without any warning or permission...

Death comes...

All the above death affirmations went through my mind and spirit soon after I arrived in Texas, soon after it dawned on me that I was alone, living alone, taking care of me, alone, and just being, alone...

While in Texas, right before going to sleep, in my bedroom, all alone, in the dark, the worst all-encompassing fear was that of getting the news of one of my parents passing... I would pray, wake up with my heart pounding, cry and pray again, all while avoiding the admission of my impotence vis-à-vis such an inevitable predicament... I can still remember how appeased I would feel when my parents would call me over the weekend, during the regular weekly call, and I would hear the voices of both my father and mother...

Aloneness and death are very similar, very simple to observe and yet very hard to accept and digest their ramifications...

Alone, for over a year at a time, away from home, was very hard. The hardest part was celebrating Christmas and Easter away, alone, trying to pretend that the next day would be better, trying to pretend that soon I would see my loved ones again, pretending and pretending and more pretending... And, as I went to sleep again, I would try to avoid the pain inside, the deafening sound of aloneness inside, the anxiety of never seeing them again, with all the risks of war, death, health, unknowns and more unknowns...

1994

One day in November 1993, while in Austin, Texas, I received a call from my family back home that my father was in the hospital, gravely ill. When he returned home, I talked to my father, and I sensed something was very wrong, something that transcended the call, something that smelled of death approaching. After the call, my stomach cramped, my system chocked up, and I went to my bed with tears in my eyes. I sensed my father was dying… I could not make sense of my instinctive feelings, but inside, my heart felt it all through the call, the voice, the tone, the energy… I wanted to face the truth, but could not, as I was facing another form of death, that of a relationship with a woman who had lived with me for more than two years then.

Facing two deaths at the same time was hard, surreal, and all engulfing. My system was sinking in anxieties, emotions, states I have never experienced before, states I was never trained nor equipped to deal with… It was as if I were born again each day, trying to learn how to walk, how to breathe, how to communicate, and all without the ability to ask for help, or ask time to slow down the escalation of pain, the downhill journey into the abyss of my own subconscious fears, addictions, attachments, needs, selfishness, and more and much more…

The ultimate death journey, death fight, death acceptance, death transcendence, death dance had just begun. Overwhelmed with the complexity of emotions, the interlinking of pains, the art of listening to death approaching, I started meditating. I needed some sort of escape to stop or temper my brain, my anxieties, my emotions, my thoughts from racing… I needed to calm my addictions to moments, to faces, to smells, to energies, to feelings, to sanity… I needed to be, to be one with life, at least to prepare me for the deaths to come… I started to walk and listen to nature, to birds, to ants, to leaves, to steps... I started learning to calm the spirit, to calm the unknowns, to calm all that was out of my control...

I started writing...

Writing was my savior, and my sanity check... I wrote my pain inside my laptop... I wrote my thoughts, as raw as they were... Writing was the exorcism of pain inside my heart, my spirit, my body, my soul... Writing was helping me deal with me, with my own fears, with my own inability to deal with death, my own impotence vis-à-vis its visits, or planned visits, and the ultimate losses that would ensue...

I wrote daily, morning, night, late night, whenever I could, and whenever I needed to... My laptop was my companion through this journey, with over two thousand pages logged, documenting the pain, the moments, the existential reality I was facing and trying to adjust to, trying to deal with and stop, if I could... Through my laptop, I was talking to me, to God, to the world, to my father, to my family, to my friends, to my partner and her parents, to my spirit...

I thought of visiting death many times, of arranging my eternal journey many times, of checking out many times... Oh how painful the journey with death was, and had been for me to endure, to move through...

Death was and is never forgiving, and always determined, without mercy nor realistic expectations...

In December 1993, my partner moved back home with her parents in Massachusetts, and it was the last time I saw her... We talked a few times in 1993 and 1994, after which I never heard from her again... The process of her dying in my life had begun earlier, but dealing with it simultaneously with the imminent death of my father was very hard. I did not have time to understand, to comprehend, to transcend, to deal with each emotion separately... I did not have the luxury of asking or influencing either of the two 'deaths' to stop, to slow down...

I desperately needed to be with my father, my sweet and best friend of a father, my eternal soul friend of a father...

The day we decided to call the whole thing off was on January 12, 1994, the same day I learned of my father's true illness — pancreatic cancer, i.e. imminent death. The simultaneous deaths were surreal then. I cried profusely at the thought of losing my father, as his illness was a condemnation to die — at that time, the one-year survival rate for pancreatic cancer was less than five per cent.

By ending the relationship, I was free, albeit partially, to face the developing illness inside my father's body, and focus on his eternal journey. As the family decided to seek cancer treatment for my father in Houston, Texas, I began preparing the terrain in Houston for the arrival in February 1994 of my father, and the family. Houston had, and still has, one of the best cancer centers in the world. We initiated contact with a reputable doctor, and he was a master spirit healer, more so than a cancer healer.

My father, who had lost more than thirty kilograms, was not the father I had known all my life... When I saw him at the airport, wearing his rain coat and beige hat, I was shocked, completely and utterly, but pretended not to have noticed anything unusual.

He walked through the airport gate frowning, as if to send fear in the spine of death, as if to tell death that he is coming after it, coming to get healed, coming to have a new beginning... And how sweet it was to kiss and hug him then.

With his face yellowish pale, I smelled death hovering around him when I kissed him… How surreal it was to pretend and lie then, to stay silent inside and hide the pain, the fear, the sight of death approaching, the smell of death filling the airport, my brain, my lungs, my heart, my eyes, my ears, my spirit…

All the family joined in, albeit intermittently, including my youngest uncle whom my father had raised after my grandfather's early passing, and whom I considered as my third and eldest brother. With the full team ready, we began preparing the treatment journey, assigning tasks, coordinating with doctors, nurses, laboratories, and all the other tasks that needed daily attention.

The family was wired with non-communication, non-sharing of emotions; we were all pretending as if things were going to get better… And, deep down, we felt that we transferred this energy to my father, as we knew he was ready…

If anyone could pull off this fight with cancer, with death, and win, it was him…

After the major tests were performed, the biggest shock was that my father's cancer had metastasized to his liver, with several cancer spots already showing. The doctors and radiologists in Lebanon failed to identify and diagnose such metastasis, unfortunately. The news killed us within, as it reduced my father's chances of surmounting this cancer — our chances to fight on — to zero.

With a new reality, absorbing the shock, the denial, the anxiety, the stomach and liver cramps, the indigestions, the panic attacks, the screams, the imminent death was severely excruciating… The art of lying to my father about the actual state of his cancer became the name of the game…

We tried to hide it in front of him, but when we were alone, reality would set in, and we would cry… I remember my younger brother and I sitting in my father's bedroom, both of us smelling his hat and crying… We started missing him before he was gone, we started accepting the reality of his passing, we started our journey of goodbyes, albeit subtle, but very real within.

Soon after the metastasis discovery, the cycles of chemotherapy began, and my father started responding beautifully. With Easter right around the corner, my father's positive response to the treatment coincided with Christ's resurrection. Such a spiritual association was mixed with Orthodox chants and ceremonies at home… Hope was hovering all around, and the doctor kept on pumping up my father's and the family's morale, as if to fight death approaching with a gang of hope and extreme optimism…

The journey had its fun-filled days as well, with trips to the golf club, with an evening at the flamenco club — my father's favorite western/eastern music and dance, with trips to exotic restaurants, with family sessions filled with jokes, with music, with chants, with laughter, with deep conversations with my father…

Throughout this journey, I was so exhausted; I would sleep whenever I could, on the floor at the doctor's, on sofas, on beds at the hospital… My vigilance was at its highest, as on numerous occasions, I caught several mistakes by nurses that could have caused my father's imminent death…

And all through these cycles, I was writing my silent pains through the nights, typing away on my laptop, documenting my pain with my fingers, getting in touch with my own sanity, centering me, preparing me for what was to come, the unknown, death and much more...

We were very optimistic and proud of our father, but very wary inside. One day in May, I sat down with the doctor, and he laid the truth on me... He literally explained that my father was near death and all we were doing was delaying it, delaying the onset, and hoping for a few more months in the fight... Hearing this killed me inside as I was starting to believe in a miracle, the power of hope in making a change in the cycle of death we were on.

In June, the blood tests were showing good signs, but the liver stent started to clog, thus escalating the interventions of a stent change, and several of them, and the cycle escalated... We spent the whole month in the hospital, on and off...

With my father's health deteriorating, we decided it was time to fly him back to Lebanon, and arranged for such a flight with a nurse accompanying the whole family. It was mid-July, and I decided to stay back for a few days in order to close down the Houston 'cancer headquarters' before joining the family back in Beirut. At the airport, while saying goodbye to my father, I remember hugging and kissing him so hard, and after they rolled him through the gates on the wheelchair, after saying goodbye, after sitting alone with my pain, with my rage, with my failure to stop death from reaching him, I started crying like I never had before in my life...

I just felt it was the final leg of our 'death journey'... It was a moment of eternal screams, cries to the gods, cries to life, cries to death to be merciful... Oh how hard this was... I waited for the airplane to take off, and went back home, alone, with my back 'broken' and the silent sounds and echoes of death all around me, accompanying me, knocking me out and around, mutilating the energy of hope I had inside... I was walking like a zombie, lifeless, hopeless, dreamless… I was walking with death, all while death was enjoying the feast, enjoying the win, enjoying the rage inside me, enjoying my impotence in front of its wrath…

A few days later, I joined my father and the family in Lebanon, in the hospital. With very long hair, with very deep pain, and with an omnipresent humorous self, I was making jokes, making light of things…

The deeper the pain is, the lighter and sweeter the humor…

Pain is the oxygen of humor… It gives it spice, depth, and dimension…

Humor caresses pain, and lightens the blow…

And how bizarre it is when laughter echoes pain, and vice versa…

I remember my father's doctor at the St. Georges Hospital in Beirut asking me what it was that I did in life, with my long hair and humorous demeanor, and my come-back answer was that I was a betting gambler at the horse track — 'Bil3ab bil Saba8'… The doctor was offended by my 'non-serious' response, and dismissed me, my presence, altogether.

Over the following month, my father's health deteriorated; his cancer was ravaging his body, eating him inside-out, poisoning his system, mutilating his face, his legs, his stomach, his fingers… His breath was slow and shallow, and his eyes, his piercing big eyes looking at us, at me, as if asking me to do something, me the impotent son in front of this ravaging illness, as if asking me to save him, to bring hope… And then, one day, my father spoke to me: "Let God's will be done… There are bigger calamities my son… calm down…" Hearing those statements calmed me down, as I realized he had started accepting his death, his end, and helping me accept it as well, helping all of us transcend it with him in order to help him…

How grand this was to watch, to hear, to feel… Instead of me helping him, he was helping me, helping all of us… He was my giant soul pillar until the last minute…

Twenty-four hours before his death in August, his doctor told us that my father's condition was worsening and that his death was imminent. It was then that I told the doctor about why I responded the way I did a few weeks earlier…

"I was at the races with death, competing with death to see who would get to my father first… I tried to win and save my father, but from what you're saying, it seems that I lost, and death will get to my father before me…"

When the doctor heard those words, he looked down, apologized for his reaction a month earlier, and we shook hands…

The night before his death, I slept in an adjacent room at the hospital with my uncle… I could not sleep that night, tossing and turning, knowing that I was spending my last day/hours/minutes/seconds with my father… I was scared, yet determined to face it, masking my fears… I was crying, and yet masking my tears… I hated to wait, to watch death enjoying the feast, to admit my impotence, to surrender, to be silent with lies, to numb my rage… I simply hated it with all my heart… My silent screams of anger and deceit were immense, all welled up inside me, inside every breath… My inner silence was deafening, more painful than any words could describe...

At dawn of that Thursday morning, August 18, 1994, my uncle and I woke up and went to see my father... He was having a hard time breathing, his eyes facing upwards, his lungs barely filling up with oxygen, his eyes bulging and yellow from the liver poisoning... I asked him if I could do anything for him, and he nudged his head up as if to say no... I caressed his head and kissed his face, and my uncle and I went down to the ground floor of the hospital to plan his funeral with the hospital management... At 9.05 a.m., I started choking up while talking to my uncle and the hospital team. I bent forward on the desk and asked all present to stop talking as I was having extreme difficulty breathing. While they were asking me about my state, the executive assistant came into the office to inform us that my father had just died!

Death came by while I was away and snatched my father right out... Oh how cowardly of death to do so... His sixty-one-year-old spirit was fighting, and still clinging... His spirit was going through me, clinging, as if asking me for help...

O Walid, the impotent in front of death... O Walid, where were you? My father's spirit was clinging till the last minute, all while my uncle and I started running seven floors up to go see him, see what was left of him... See what was left of us in him... See...

When I saw him, with taped eyes, taped mouth, lying there on his bed, still, peaceful, serene, silent, sweet, I ran screaming at him, calling him to come back to me, calling him to stay, at least for a while more, until I could face him, face death with both him and me present...

I stayed with him, his body, his still warm body, all through the embalming, all the way till they powdered him, and got him ready for the freezer... The death freezer was a surreal sight, with small death chambers, filled with still and dead bodies... What a sight that was!

The death freezer felt as the death store, where bodies wait their turn to be escorted out to their final resting place...

After this inner and outer body incident, after this encounter with death, after this lost fight with death, after this silent butchering of my father's spirit and mine, I was looking forward to the death ceremony, the death festival, the death march...

At church, with several bishops performing the death ceremony, all I could focus on was the brown coffin where my father was... I could not believe that he was inside it, lying there, motionless, dead... Just imagining such a state was overwhelming, let alone the sight of him, at the end of the death prayers, where the bishops lifted the coffin's cover, and placed sand on his mouth, and sacred oil on his body... Such a ritual was and still is eerie, rooted within the Christian beliefs of 'Ashes to Ashes, Dust to Dust' and how the body will morph, disintegrate back to dust, after death...

My father's body was finally ready for the death feast, for death to savor every flesh and bone left of him...

With joy and rage, I joined the death march, the death celebration, the death ceremony... I could not wait to march with my father to his final resting place, to his grave, to my grave... Wearing a white suit, a white hat, along with my brothers, sister, and the whole Touma family, we marched and marched, behind a dancing coffin to the tunes of the death symphony played by the death band, the brass horns singing tunes I have heard so many times before, but never knew how it was to feel them with such pain...

The photo of my father ahead of the convoy, a convoy several thousand people strong, decided to take a detour to visit the Arak Touma manufacturing plant... In there, the coffin tap-danced with joy at the sight, and the plant welcomed my father and all of us as if to chant its final goodbyes with us...

In there, on my grandmother's porch where I danced with death in the 1976 war, I took the same machine gun I had carried then and fired tens of rounds in the air, rounds of extreme pain and rage, rounds of screams to the gods for such a generous offering they just received, the offering of our father, our leader, our pillar, our healer, our friend, our giant, our sweet lamb...

We continued on to the graveyard, entered the big black gate, and headed to the family mausoleum... The family mausoleum was covered with white stones, with a plaque on it: Family of Tanos Gibran Touma...

The red gate of the mausoleum was open, with a sinister darkness spewing from within, smiling to receive its first eternal visitor, its first eternal resident...

My father's coffin was the first to caress the floor of the family mausoleum, placed in the left corner, in silence, in peace, in serenity, in stillness... My uncle closed the mausoleum door, and hid the keys...

After that day, my father never left me...

After that day, death never left me...

After that day, life never left me, for now at least...

1994 to Date

Many times, I wanted to go open the mausoleum's door and check on my father... My uncle would not give me those keys... I would visit the graveyard though, regularly, bringing my father flowers, candles, water, my prayers, my tears, my wishes, my stories, my pains, my nostalgia, my longing, my eternal dreams...

After that day, my grandmother and two of my uncles became eternal residents of this mausoleum, the very welcoming and peaceful mausoleum, filling it up nicely... Soon this mausoleum will run out of space, as the death feasts will need more space to welcome the very serene residents of the Tanos Gibran Touma family...

Deaths... Many a Form

Endings are hard, more than death sometimes...

Endings are complicated and difficult to deal with and rationalize, irrespective what form or shape they take...

Both deaths and endings are synonymous in certain cases. The object of death or ending could be abstract, surreal, material, emotional, spiritual, physical — all forms that we might feel or experience through life, and yet each one of us deals with each ending, or form of death, in her/his own way... And each one of us describes the feelings involved with the ending in her/his way, through the dimension that suits her/him...

Of the many forms of endings and/or deaths, what follows is a simple list of some forms, albeit non-exhaustive, but cuts through many an experience we faced/face/will face in life:

Death of childhood, of puberty, of adolescence, of adulthood...

Death of relationships, of friendships...

Death of marriage, of partnerships...
Death of jobs, of engagements, of commitments...
Death of simplicity, of maturity...
Death of inner calm, of serenity, of peace...
Death of control, of manipulation...
Death of needs, of addictions...
Death of hormones, of cells, of senses...
Death of body organs, of sexuality...
Death of memories, of recollections, of history...
Death of love, of feelings, of emotions...
Death of karma at the door of clearance...
Death of the tongue, of language...
Death of light, of clarity...
Death of hope, of aspirations, of ambitions...
Death of fear, of anxiety, of hesitation...
Death of past, of present, of future...
Death of imagination, of thought, of creativity, of genius...
Death of moments...
Death of time...
Death of spirit...
Death of death...
Death...

As listed above, the deaths in form are real, but their core substance is so unique, and each with its own taste and shape... Moreover, some of these deaths or endings may only be temporary and one may rekindle their underlying energy... As such, the above deaths are painful, but not terminal in terms of ending life, per se.

However, I am sure that the above deaths can be so

personal and so hard that one would wish life to end at times rather than endure such pains, such deaths, without any control over feelings, emotions, or thoughts overwhelming us during the death cycle.

At times, spiritual or emotional deaths are necessary in order for us to move on and rekindle hope with a new cycle in life...

Death is rebirth, rejuvenation, newness, freshness...

Death is another form of life, and is and can be a source of life...

Such dichotomy of ending and beginning, death and life, is real and very much part of the transformational energy that is death, death the other face or form of life, death the metamorphosis, death the transformer...

Death... My Friend

And I dare ask why I am an existentialist at heart! And I dare ask why I am one with death! And I dare confirm that I taste death every day! And I dare affirm that I die every day a little! And I dare assert that I danced with death many a time in my life!

O, Death... You have been lurking around all my life, tickling me, toying with me, reminding me daily that you are coming, right around the corner, waiting for the right time to take me, to bring my body home to my eternal resting place... As a cancer survivor, you knocked on my door a few years back but decided it is not yet time to take me 'home'... And now, with high blood pressure and atrial fibrillation, my heart is dancing to your march, 'the death march', with rhythms I've never heard before, rhythms of rejoicing drums, all catapulting my awareness of the now, all while daring to breathe slowly, peacefully, and yet, sadly. Sad, I am, that your silence is getting closer and closer, and knocking at my door, my life... Oh well, I am ready for the fight, till the last beat... With peace, I will go... With peace, I will fight... With peace, I will be...

My body will spend more time with you, death, than living on this earth... As such, befriending you is to my body's advantage and getting used to you is healthy for my body as well... Or so my body assumes... Freeing my spirit, at least, from your impending call helps me enjoy the moment... Sharing my time on earth with your sitting on my shoulders, observing, appeases me for a while, and makes of you an eternal, merciful friend... I hope...

O Death, my dear friend...

How I despise and hate you...

How merciless a friend you can be... And will be...

I am and will be waiting for our eternal encounter...

For now... I bid you peace, my friend...

And for a while, I hope...

Positive Friction

We rub off on each other... Consequently, we might co-ride the karmic cycles of those closest to us. The crossing of our karmic cycles with those closest to us may well cause friction and amplify the impact of our cycles on each other's lives... Be they positive or negative, the lack of awareness of the effect of such friction could cause pain to both parties, pain due to miscommunication, pain due to the lack of awareness of the extent that such friction is having on them, on their relationship...

Positive friction is when we are aware of our karmic cycles crossing another's, and we strive to calmly move them forward, free their negative effects on one another, and keep the positive energy flowing with those closest to us.

Do Good...

Do Good... and Beware...

> Beware of those you have done good to...
> Beware the person who has received charity from you...

Positive friction, and all the goodwill associated with it, can easily be weaponized by the receiving party, out of weakness, out of an insecure spirit not able to receive good from the initiating party. Mind you, the receiving party needs the positive friction of the initiating party, and needs the initiating party to stand by them and be the donor per se.

Such a contradictory response is very disturbing and can be discouraging from the point of view of the giver — the positive friction initiator, the contributor of goodwill... As if one should never do good so that one does not receive evil in return!

However, if we truly believe in karma and its manifestations within our lives, when one does good, one is riding the karmic cycle of the receiver and allowing the receiver to ride their own karmic cycle... As such, the karmic cycles of the donor and the receiver cross with a risk of such intertwinement ricocheting the negative effects of the receiver on the donor. Accordingly, the statement 'beware of those you have done good to' is an authentic warning and very much true in implementation.

When a spirit is poor, nothing satisfies it... And such poor spirits will poison any initiative of positive friction.

Stale, poor, and arid spirits will exude negative friction by nature, and such individuals' poisonous orbit and karmic cycles should be avoided, when possible... If not avoidable, minimizing interaction or friction with them is a must...

Positive friction is a natural manifestation of societal bonding for the majority of human beings. Creating bonds with those closest to us is sought after and brings a lot of satisfaction and completeness to society. However, being aware of who we are 'riding' with, the karmic cycle they carry with them, is a critical eye-opener for us to complete our cycle without causing our innate will for positive friction to transform into a negative inward spiral and deter us from giving.

Do Good... and Smile...

Do good and karma will do the rest...

Positive friction is an act of goodwill, an act of positive intentions, an act of giving par excellence. One cannot fake being good, or doing good... The karmic cycle will always expose the good from the bad, as bad cycles back and so does good...

Doing good, riding the positive friction of the karmic cycle, all while planting the seeds of goodwill, good intentions, will always launch on the giver's cycle a positive energy that will come back in folds... And such is the positive energy amplification in one's life, in the echoing of positive goodwill coming back to bathe the giver and all in her/his orbit...

Inner Peace

As one becomes aware of the cycles of karma, and how each cycle affects both her/him and those in one's orbit, a deeply satisfying state ensues. Positive friction becomes a deep state of awareness and consciousness, a state of generous being and giving, a state of peace within.

Such state of inner peace comes from centering the spirit,

from being one with it, one with the journey, one with the positive frictions that we need to plant in order to complete the life cycle we are born with.

Deep inner peace is:

- Truth
- Inner calm
- Serenity within
- Clear conscience
- Emancipated spirit
- Clean heart
- Vibrant spirit
- Elevated spirit
- Aware spirit
- Pure spirit

Our dance with positive frictions is an ever-winding loop within life, and with life... It is our duty to make of inner peace a driver for truth and serenity within, for increasing our awareness, for serving others, for purifying our soul and spirit, and, simply, for being...

Vows:

The Dance with Eternity

Impetus

At their core, vows are a form of worship, a commitment of some sort. Sometimes vows are the echo of repentance, other times a security blanket, an assurance between humans and the metaphysical spiritual realm, the God realm, or whatever spiritual form or gods those making and fulfilling the vows are comfortable with.

At times, vows take the form of an offering. Such offerings could go back thousands of years through traditional fulfillment over the ages, all in the hope of appeasing the gods, soliciting their mercy, adhering to their will. Each offering has a unique form that reflects the indigenous beliefs and traditions of the region where it is being fulfilled. For instance, an offering could be in the form of a monetary donation, lit candles, burnt incense, planted flowers, slain lambs, goats, or bulls at the offering site, and many other forms that cultures over the ages have adopted to fulfill their committed vows.

On a deeper level, offerings are made in return for some inner faith, inner belief that the gods will take care of and protect the families of the mortals making the offerings, the mortals fulfilling their vows, clearing their karma and those of their loved ones... On another level, offerings may be made on the basis of superstition and the compulsive nature of the individual performing them in order to alleviate the superstitious associations lodged in her/his psyche, and the observed and learned behavior from the ancestors over the ages.

At their roots, vows are a response to the impotence of spirits in front of death.

Vows and offerings secure an assurance from evil, from ill will, from death, albeit temporary and deceitfully disguised... Vows are an indemnity with God, with Jesus, with the Holy Virgin Mary, with Saints, with Prophets, with the Buddha, with the gods, with all good-givers and eternally present and potent powers of the spiritual sphere, the protectors from harm... Or so the makers of the vows believe...

In repeatedly fulfilling the vows and completing the offerings, the vows become family traditions, traditions as communion with the family's fate, the family's eternal path. Those vows are repeated as often as we believe is needed, as often as our fear of retribution from the angry spirits necessitates, as often as we need to feel comfortable with the delaying of our end, and that of our loved ones... Or so we desperately hope and want to believe...

Vows are an affirmation of our weakness in front of endings, our fears of endings, our rejection of endings...

With vows, we bow in front of our own death, ask for forgiveness from God, or whomever we believe to be both life giver and life taker…

With vows and offerings, we forgive life, life's creator, for making us mortals, for the death sentence imposed upon us since birth…

With vows and offerings, we plant seeds of love and care, eternally send good karma, and innocently expect it back — hopefully in our lifetime.

With vows and offerings, we forgive ourselves, we wash our pain, we clear our past, we pave goodwill for our future…

Deep down, vows echo our fear of the pain of loss… We keep on offering and offering to calm such fears, for a while at least, to calm our impotence, for a while at least, to calm our lack of control, to calm our own death callings, for a while at least, and so we hope…

With vows and offerings, we forgive death… For a while, at least…

Eternal Vows: My Great Grandfather's Story

I was born into a Greek Orthodox family, totally indoctrinated in the Christian faith, with very strict vows performed by the family for five generations to date at the Lady of Saydnaya Monastery in Syria.

It all started in the late nineteenth century and the events that ensued in the early twentieth century when my great grandfather made the following vows to the Lady of Saydnaya: a) every granddaughter and grandson born in his family tree and their offspring will be baptized at the Lady of Saydnaya Monastery, and b) every grandson and all male offspring will keep their hair uncut until they are four years old, at which age the nuns of the Lady of Saydnaya Monastery cut their hair and the weight of the hair in gold is donated to the Monastery.

Basically, every newborn child in my great grandfather's family lineage was interlocked with either one or two of these vows; as mandated by the Christian Orthodox faith, these vows had to be made, regardless of the difficulty the parents may experience in carrying them out, including getting to the Monastery, and preforming the rituals within the time restrictions.

When I enquired with family relatives as to why my great grandfather made such solemn and eternal vows, their impetus and foundation were quite dark and grim.

My great grandfather and great grandmother lived together in a home on top of and near the old and current Arak Touma factories, respectively. They had four daughters and three sons.

In the early 1900s and right around the First World War, my great grandmother violated the trust of my great grandfather and greatly disappointed him. Angry and deceived, my great grandfather decided to leave the house, leave my great grandmother, and go live in the vineyard from which the grapes were harvested to make Arak Touma, the vineyard where he, one of his daughters, and my grandfather are now buried. My great grandfather made of the vineyard an eternal resting place for the family and locked its meaning and spiritual value within and for the family so that no one would sell it as it was a source of much-needed income during the days of famine in the early 1900s.

My great grandfather's treatment of his wife after this incident was very detrimental to her, and she died not long after. Three of their daughters married, and one remained single. The marriages were not successful, with a very dramatic turn of events facing each one of them, each with her husband… It was as if their karma were interwoven with the karma of their mother, all carrying the pain and existential karma of their parents.

With such bad karma befalling his married daughters and the problems and pains he had experienced with his late wife, my great grandfather made these vows to the Lady of Saydnaya, the guardian of the Touma family and to the Monastery which he visited many times on his mule. Intentionally, my great grandfather made the vows far more onerous on the boys; in addition to being baptized at the Monastery, each boy had to go four years after birth without cutting his hair. This meant that he would look like a girl for a while with his long hair, be picked on by other boys, be subject to endless questions of why, go many days without either washing or braiding it out of rebellion towards such predicament, and then, suddenly, at the age of four, have his hair chopped off at the Monastery.

My great grandfather's vows were a form of remorse, a form of sorrow for the ill fate that had befallen his daughters, a form of penitence for the inner family karma with his wife and daughters, a bow to the pain and the associated karma that ensued and affected his family so harshly.

Maybe my great grandfather was sorry for what he did to his wife, maybe he was sorry for holding on to such pain for so long and for letting it cripple the women of his family... maybe... All conjectures as I never knew him nor talked to him about such pain... And such a depiction of his pain is but my own perception, unfortunately...

Today, the family's commitment to the vows is unwavering by every member of my great grandfather's family, without questioning, just performing... out of respect, honor, and eternal pledge.

On some level, the vows are performed without understanding the deep pains that triggered such eternal commitment, performed out of fear of retribution by the spirit of the vow holder or maker, out of subconscious guilt, out of fear of the roaming spirits of ancestors, observing spirits, judging spirits, waiting spirits, crying spirits, sad spirits, merciful spirits, forgiving spirits, tender spirits... spirits... On a spiritual level, the vows are performed out of respect for the intricate feelings and thoughts that make of the relationship with the Lady of Saydnaya the choice it is within the Touma family right now, in the now where every member is, or might be, around the world, inside her/his heart, within her/his soul.

I am sure that if all the family understood the depth of pain our great grandfather felt, the vows will become karma cleansing acts that would be performed out of respect and out of remorse... And the cycle would be cleansed for generations to come, all in oneness for the greater good of the family and its internal dynamics.

Notes...

The Lady of Saydnaya, or Shaghoura, has phenomenal powers over and presence within the Touma family psyche, family bonds, communion with and in front of God, in front of our conscience... The Shaghoura has attained an overarching identity as the eternal mother of all, eternal companion, savior, healer, guardian... Almost every car carries an icon from the Monastery, every house displays icons, incense, oil, and all kinds of 'guardian tools and affirmations' related to the individual's rapport with the Lady of Saydnaya, with 'taught and observed behavior', with nostalgia, with memories of our grandmother, our fathers, our mothers, our uncles, our aunts, our brothers, our sisters, our families, all triggering moments that make of the Shaghoura an omnipresent spirit that make of the Lady of Saydnaya our eternal mother, our guardian and the guardian of our family and our offspring...

The eternal chain of vows is all encompassing and intimidating, but oh so very sweet, endearing, and deep in meaning, in bonds, in care, in being... Just being at peace with both past and present and with what is yet to come is in itself enough to make such eternal bonds that much lighter, that much more imbued with serenity and eternal peace... The family bond born of such vows breaks all barriers and makes of the family lineage a far deeper bond than money, business, or material wealth could ever create...

On some level, these vows are very endearing, and yet, very scary... What if one fails to fulfill them, for whatever reason? What if? What would happen to her/his family? What would happen to her/his child(ren)? What would be the karmic cycle ramifications? Such existential fulfillment and guilt are very hard to bear when one commits to being part of this family, part of my great grandfather's karma clearing cycle, part of the eternal bond that unites families around such vows, such rituals, such forms of worship of a higher being, such forms of guilt and karma cleansing...

The Monastery

Founded in the sixth century, around 547 AD, the Lady of Saydnaya Monastery is about thirty kilometers north of Damascus in Syria. Located on the hill in the village of Saydnaya, the Monastery looks like a fortress with its walls, its domes, its gates, its windows, its stairs, its church bells, all towering over the village like a guardian from the skies, omnipresent, omnipotent... What an impressive Monastery it is, still, and will be for ages to come.

The Monastery was the seat of the ancient Patriarchate of Antioch and is dedicated to the Nativity of the Holy Virgin Mary, Theotokos, or Mother of God. The Monastery is considered by many to be second to Jerusalem in religious significance to the Christian faith. Notably, the Monastery is visited today by both Christians and Muslims as the Lady of Saydnaya has been revered for her generous miracles and healing powers over the ages, across all walks of life, faiths, and religious sects.

Led by an Abbess, the Monastery is occupied and managed by nuns, all in black or navy dresses and headscarves, with a very unique demeanor and appearance. My father's cousin was a nun at the Monastery; she lived in and served at the Monastery until she passed away several decades ago. The nuns are mostly orphans who lived and studied at the Monastery and its associated school. Some of them have very distinct voices, distinct prayer styles that are very unique to the Lady of Saydnaya Monastery psyche, aura, and flare. Their voices still resonate in my ears, and I long to hear them, to listen to them, to bask in their prayer mantras, their chants, their communication with God and the Holy

Virgin Mary... They rarely smile, but one can feel they serve with dignity, honor, love, and genuineness, all in the name of the Holy Virgin Mary, or *3Adra* as they call her.

Over the years, my wife, our children, and I have developed a beautiful relationship with the Abbess and four beautiful spirits, solid nuns and servants of the Shaghoura, solid orphans and soldiers of the cause — the Lady of Saydnaya cause...

Upon reaching the Monastery, there are a series of winding stairs that were built in the mid-twentieth century, an elevator, and a very old stone walkway up, all leading to the main gate of the Monastery. The gate is not high, built of large stones like a cavern inside the Monastery's towering front wall... I always had to bow my head to enter. Symbolically, this bow is very humbling as one enters such a holy place...

As you enter this Monastery, the brushed, soft, and shiny rocks underneath your feet, the brushed and soft wall stones to your left and right, all recite the stories of centuries past, of the millions of hands and feet of pilgrims caressing this holy place, making their journey for worship, for vow fulfillment, for healing, for inner peace, for 'preparation of what is to come'. All journeys in communion with the Holy Virgin Mary, referred to as the Shaghoura of the Monastery, the 'Celebrated', the 'Renowned'.

As you climb the stairs and go deeper inside the Monastery, you sense its unique architecture, its unique smell of the food being prepared by the nuns, its unique smell of incense and candles burning in the main Church, and the very holy shrine of the Virgin Mary Icon, the Shaghoura... The common belief at the Monastery is that the icon of the Holy Virgin Mary, the Shaghoura, is one of four icons painted by St.

Luke the Evangelist, and brought to the Monastery at the request of Abbess Marina in the late eighth century.

The Gazelle

When crossing the Syrian desert with his army during the sixth century AD, Justinian the Great, Emperor of Byzantium, set up camp near what is known today as the town of Saydnaya. Soon, he and his troops began to suffer from dehydration. While looking for a water hole, a spring, Justinian saw a gazelle off in the distance and followed it in the hope of hunting it for food, or that it may lead him to a water source in the desert they were in. While chasing the gazelle, the emperor saw it stop on a rocky mount and approach a spring of fresh water. As Justinian approached and prepared to kill the gazelle, the gazelle suddenly transformed into an icon of the Holy Mother of God, the Holy Theotokos, and gleamed with a brilliant light. From the shining icon, a white hand stretched and a voice asked him to not kill the gazelle and to build a church on the mount where the gazelle was drinking water. When the divine light disappeared, Justinian returned to his troops, recounted what had happened with the gazelle, and ordered them to start the plans to build a church on the Saydnaya mount.

The architects struggled to develop the church plans and the Holy Virgin Mary reappeared as the gazelle in Justinian's dream, and shared the plans of what would become the Lady of Saydnaya Monastery, and of which she would be the guardian.

The gazelle, the interlink with the Holy Virgin Mary, the Lady of Saydnaya Monastery, the legacy of what has become today the holiest of shrines for my family to visit for worship over the past three centuries, deeply affected my great grandfather who made the Gazelle the main logo of the Arak Touma brand, from 1888 to date.

As a child, working in the arak plant, I grew up looking at the gazelle on labels, on boxes, on stickers; it was and still is part of every image and logo utilized for Arak Touma... Effectively, the gazelle became synonymous and symbolic of the Arak Touma brand, a communion of some sort with what Arak Touma symbolizes to the Touma family, a link to both the spiritual and emotional heritage the Monastery represents today, a link between generations...

The Church

The church of the Monastery is quite impressive, and busy... Busy with icons adorning its walls, its pillars, its ceilings, its doors... Busy with candles, with incense holders, with its wooden iconostasis, seats, and chairs... Busy with prayers... Busy with baptisms, godfathers and godmothers, children and parents crying before and after the baptism, grandparents taking pictures and crying as well, busy with priests performing such baptisms with the utmost of diligence, efficiency, script, and very violent execution...

Baptism and Orthodoxy

Baptism is a sacrament in Christianity, a rite of passage, a rite of indoctrination, a rite of restoring real life (or so we are told), a rite of belonging to the Christian 'community' as founded by Jesus after his resurrection... Ultimately, this sacrament has become a critical ritual for every family, every child born within a Christian family... And such a ritual has to be performed during a certain period for the child to become 'part of the church, part of the community', reject the original 'sin'… Or better yet, cleanse the original guilt, free the control chains that religions are and can be… Or better yet, put on new chains, but with different labels, colors, tenacity, and meaning…

In order to become a member of the ecclesiastical family of Jesus, one has to reject 'evil', both initiator and instigator of sin, and become one with Jesus… Such is the Christian indoctrination, and such is the limitation of any faith, or religion… The spiritual realm in such cases becomes tied to 'material' and symbolic behavior, albeit important in meaning, it can become demeaning in its implementation over the ages.

We perform such rituals while ignoring that evil is within us, each one of us, and we have to recognize it, and deal with it on a conscious level, with full awareness of our weaknesses, with full awareness that we will err, that we will succumb to 'sin and evil', and that it is all part of being human, with or without being religious, irrespective of the faith…

I am certain very few baptisms have the depth of sacrament as mentioned above, and very few participants understand the underlying meaning behind each step as delineated below… Most participants in such sacraments just go with the flow, and do it out of due process, as a ceremonial family event with church as the venue, as a new type of engagement for celebrations…

Religions and their associated sacraments must redefine the spiritual relationships that exist today with worshippers, the family and societal bonds, and what a church represents, the role of priests, the role of sacraments, the role of vows, the role of religious bonds, be they eternal or temporary, but bond structures nonetheless...

After all, religion at birth is not a choice, but implementing the teachings of religions when one grows up and matures is a choice. As such, the church, and all world religions for that matter, are at very tough crossroads, and have to define what such choices mean for the individual, the family, society, the country, the world.

In today's networked world, social media can easily manipulate the truth, redefine the impetus behind any religious vow, meaning, act, and can easily launch massive disinformation campaigns targeted at religions and their sacraments that distort reality and make of such religions, or religious sects, the evil to avoid, all without any hard proof or facts for that matter.

The participants in an Orthodox baptism at the Lady of Saydnaya Monastery are: the priest representing Jesus, a Monastery nun, sometimes two nuns, the godfather, the godmother, and the child to be baptized. A baptism also requires a large brass basin filled with water, holy oil to add to the water, the holy Myron, towels, and candles. The audience of this ceremony comprises the family members of the child, including father and mother, brothers and sisters, grandparents and cousins if they can make it... And for sure, in the case of my family's baptisms, the audience extends to include the spirits of our great grandfather and grandmother, the spirits of their daughters, the spirits of all our grandfathers and grandmothers, the spirits of our fathers... Oh how surreal this is and will continue to be...

Baptism Steps

After the godfather records the name of the baptized in the 'Book of Life' of the Lady of Saydnaya church, and the assigned baptism name, he gives the book to the priest in order to initiate the sacrament... The assigned baptism name is usually one of a saint, revered by the child's parents.

As one of the godparents holds the child to be baptized, the priest, with half his arms bare, approaches the child and blows three times on her/his face and makes the sign of the cross while reciting 'In the name of the Father, the Son, and the Holy Spirit'... Such a step empowers the child against evil with the power of the cross, empowers the child to reject sin — for the moment at least...

The priest then puts his hand on the child's head and recites a prayer through which he asks God to keep the child under his wings, remove the old misguidance from her/him, and make the child part of the parish of Christ.

Following, the priest performs the ritual of expelling evil from the child (expelling Satan), blows in the child's face again, and asks God to keep Satan and demons away from the child in preparation for Christ to replace Satan in her/his heart...

Knowing that Satan is in the pure heart of a child, how could one look with innocence at a child again? The impetus for such sacraments, rituals, and rite of belonging needs revisiting as it might create a negative level of awareness, a strong rejection of the sacrament itself, and a strong alienation of its eternal meaning and journey for the child her/himself.

The ritual of expelling Satan starts when the priest asks the godparents, along with the child they take turns in carrying, to turn west, where west is the absence of light, the absence of good, and where evil dwells... Then, the priest asks the godparents three consecutive times: "Do you reject Satan, all his works, all his angels, all his worship and all his nobles?" The godparents, and all present, respond with: "Yes, I reject Satan", and the priest follows by asking the godparents to spout and spit on Satan, and in turn both godparents and all present spout and spit on Satan... The comic nature of this step adds some fun to the ritual itself and was indeed something we looked forward to in every baptism we attended... More so, spitting on something is immediately linked to Satan, and, as such, total rejection and annihilation... Or so we wanted to believe...

By rejecting and spitting, the child, through the godparents, is breaking the bond with hell, declaring war and starting a conflict with Satan.

What a hero-to-be this child is...! What if Satan does not exist? What if Satan will become the child when s/he grows up? Who is Satan, one might ask? And might Satan be inside a church, inside a child's spirit while getting baptized? Such existentialist questions only highlight how fragile the concepts and sacraments on which Christianity was founded are, and the fact that all of them need assessment and reassessment by the church leadership in order to tune them with the evolution of worshippers, with the expectations that such worshippers have from the church after years of practice, years of questioning, years of metamorphosing...

The rejection of Satan is a precursor to the acceptance of Christ. With the heart of the child 'pure and free from evil', the priest asks the godparents (and the child of course) to turn eastward, east where light emanates, Christ the light of the world, the light of righteousness and justice... While facing eastward, the priest asks the godparents three consecutive times whether they agree with Christ and believe in him, and they respond affirmatively, three times, and recite the Constitution of Faith "I believe in one God..." In effect, the godparents are choosing, on behalf of the child, to proclaim the doctrine of the Holy Trinity of the Father, the Son, and the Holy Spirit and invite the child to enter the Kingdom of God, to choose to be a child of God, a child of the Kingdom...

When one observes these steps of the ritual, one cannot help but wonder what is going through the child's mind, with Satan, evil, spiting, spouting, blowing, west, east, and more and more... The poor child, the innocent child has evil ripped from her/his innocent soul to be indoctrinated in Jesus, supposedly on the right path forward... Is this path the right path for the child? The right path of enlightenment? Religion becomes like a political party, a political entity, where the right of belonging is paved with all kinds of rituals to prove one deserves being in this party, part of this party, a member of this party, without one having a choice of what party to belong to, and when to belong to it... Forceful, violent steps are an understatement... Steps that could easily be met with full rejection by the child when s/he grows older and discovers that the church is no longer answering her/his spiritual questioning, no longer addressing her/his spiritual needs...

The priest then blesses the water inside the large brass basin, with all the connotations of water and what it represents in terms of good and evil, water as the source of life, source of non-corruption, a gift of sanctification, an elixir of disease, a repellant cleanser of evil.

After blessing the water, comes the moment of truth for all present, including the child, the hero of the baptism: the priest asks the godparents to take off the child's clothes. A symbolic act in reference to Adam and Eve who were naked before the fall from paradise, and also symbolic in reference to the naked Christ on the cross. Such symbolism is intense even for adults, let alone the helpless child waiting for such a rite of purification, or more aptly, a terrorize-the-soul-away-from-bad rite, or from-evil rite… for a while at least…

As the godparents undress the child, the priest recites a prayer to bless the oil before he paints it on the child's forehead, on the chest to heal both soul and body, on the ears to guide the child to hear the faith, on the hands, and finally on the feet, all to prepare the child for her/his war with Satan… *her/his war with her/his soul, spirit, desires…*

While the child is readied for what may be the greatest shock of her/his young life, while the water is being tested for its temperature, while the holy oil is being poured in, while the godparents are getting ready for their life journey with the child, holding open towels in preparation for the next step, they carry, worryingly and silently, the child… As the priest gets ready for the 'drowning', the audience turns silent, especially the mother of the child, eyes fixated on her child and mind consumed with what the priest is about to do to her/him.

The priest picks up the child for baptism, from the

godfather usually, continues the prayers until the ritual reaches the climax where the ceremony shifts into serious execution and timing... At that moment, the chills that run down the spines of every one present are palpable, felt on a collective level... *Granted that baptism cleanses Christians from their sins, but in the Orthodox Church, the baptism goes one notch higher, leaving no doubt that the evil spirit has been kicked out with a set of maneuvers that leave all in a state of awe and terror...*

The priest grabs the child, puts her/his arms behind their back, and immerses the full body of the child in a diving-motion, headfirst, in the water, in the brass basin filled with all the Touma children's memories of their own baptisms, of their subconscious experiences with this basin... The Trinity dives happen so fast, all while the child is screaming at the top of her/his lungs, screaming for help, screaming to make the process stop, looking down at the water as if to see some sort of a toy, only to be taken by surprise, drenched in disappointment, at the reality of it being nothing beyond an asphyxiating experience, never to be repeated...

"God's servant shall be baptized in the name of the Father, the Son and the Holy Spirit", says the priest during the immersions... And when the priest finishes this brutal assault on the child, on evil — or so we think, he throws the child on the godfather, with a looping motion, totally taking the godfather by surprise, who, for a second, was fully taken by the moment, by his memories in this basin, and how it might have felt like when he was baptized several decades back... A surreal few seconds of violent terrorising motions is an understatement... The child, still crying, still trying to find the comforting arms of her/his mother, is no doubt wondering what fault s/he has made, what ill s/he has done to deserve, to warrant, to justify such violent dips in water. During this entire ceremony, the mother cannot touch her child; it is the godmother who is responsible for this rite of communion with the adoption process against evil, the adoption process through life with the child — a beautiful and soulful event with the intertwinement of role and meaning...

One questions why the baptism is taking place through the immersion in water... Why not in sand, in the wind, in leaves, in ashes? Why immersion? Why not standing up with tree leaves poured over the child? Why isn't baptism the caressing of the spirit of the child? Why not the whisper and prayer for evil to leave the child alone? So many other options for such a sacrament, such a powerful family communion around one meaning, saving the child's spirit from evil, or so the faithful Christians believe... There are so many variances to such rituals, but on some level, people set them in stone over the ages, over many repetitions, over many civilizations where Christianity has spread over the past two thousand years. Is it laziness or just the 'go with the flow' mantra that makes us reconcile such differences? All questions I have no answers to at the moment, but would love to have choices if I were a child facing such acts of terror and violence on my soul while being baptized in the moment...

If baptism is the death of our selfishness and pride, well, why isn't baptism a cleansing sacrament that is performed once daily, weekly, monthly, or annually? Would it still have its glitter and anticipation? Would it still carry the power of the vow? And what if we cannot reach the Lady of Saydnaya

Monastery weekly or monthly? Very tough questions to deal with, or even try to answer, if one is locked into eternal vows, like my family is...

After the immersions, the baptized child is dressed in a white garment, symbolizing the life of the resurrection s/he has crossed, the transformation into innocence, the suit of non-corruption, non-evil, the symbol of purity, the purified soul from sin — or so we hope...

With the white dress on, the priest anoints the baptized child with the Holy Myron reciting these words: "The seal of the gift of the Holy Spirit". Such anointing, or Chrism, symbolizes the personal Pentecost of every baptized child in Christ.

After the Chrism, the godparents carry the baptized child, and the family members carry lit candles and together they circle the brass basin three times in perpetual reverence to the Holy Trinity and chant: "For all of you who are baptized into Christ, have clothed yourselves with Christ, Hallelujah"...

After reading the Gospel, the godparents advance, carrying the baptized child, to receive communion from the priest. As the baptized child takes the body and blood of Christ, the baptism is cemented, and the child is now one with Christ and the Christian Community, "partner of the divine nature," "participant of the heavenly table of the Kingdom" ...

As the last step at the church, the Holy Myron is washed away from the baptized child, with both godmother and a nun helping out in the bath... Meanwhile, the child is crying, still looking for her/his mother, longing for her help, and yet again, still, the mother is not allowed near her child in this 'adoption' phase by the godparents — tough on the mother, but symbolically powerful for the future care of the child...

On a regular day, more than a dozen baptisms take place at the Lady of Saydnaya Monastery, at blazing speeds... Amazing to watch, to be part of, to engage within...

Notes...

A vow, a ritual, a sacrament, each baptism resonates with its own meanings, and definitely, with processes well-crafted several centuries ago, with all the values surrounding every aspect of the baptism, with all the religious interpretations of every step taken while engaged in it... Twenty-first century baptisms need a solid spiritual revisit, so as to address the current nature of God as a concept in the life of every Christian, of every human trying to question the whys of such processes as imposed within religious norms and traditions.

Church Prayers

If you happen to attend Sunday morning or evening prayers, or any special holiday prayers at the Lady of Saydnaya church, well you are in luck... The chants of the church choir, composed of nuns only, will open your heart and leave you speechless as to its intensity, uniqueness, Byzantine tones, and eloquence of execution. The nuns are a joy to watch and listen to. With the Church's high ceilings and dome, and with the nuns standing in the middle of the Church around a high wooden table facing the iconostasis, the priest, and the worshippers, the echo of their chants will amplify in your spirit, and fill the whole Church with resonating tones, tones that will reverberate in your ears for many days and years to come...

The Shaghoura

Right behind the church, on the eastern side of the Monastery is a long walkway by the right side leading up to a door, to a small room where one removes shoes and sandals and enters through two small doorways, forced to enter bowing as the doorways are lower than the height of an average person, bowing to enter the most revered shrine for the Holy Virgin Mary in the world, second to Jerusalem, right there, waiting peacefully inside the Monastery's holiest space...

The Shaghoura...

A dark, small, candle-lit room with icons adorning its walls, top to bottom, all around, with a large table in the middle holding the bible for prayers conducted by a Monastery nun, with a slot for donations to the Monastery, holy oil, cotton balls to dip in the oil, candles all around, and white ribbons to place around the hand, stomach, neck, or wherever the pilgrim is asking for help, for healing, from the Shaghoura... And, there is the Shaghoura, the icon in the center of the wall, facing the praying nun, surrounded by other icons, but distinctly discreet, discreetly somber, discreetly the 'mother' of all orphans — orphan nuns serving the Monastery, discreetly the mother of all worshippers... Modest, holy in its meaning, and yet, so grand in what it represents...

Whatever God or form of God one believes in, the Shaghoura, the Holy Mother of God, the Theotokos, is all real, and all represented on this wall as an icon, emanating with energy from the humility my family's beliefs have entrusted in this icon, this room, our Shaghoura... Considering that the Holy Virgin Mary walked on earth, carried in her womb the son of God, lived by the Christian faith, witnessed almost all of Jesus' miracles and all the key 'faith' moments, such an encounter can only leave one in awe of what it represents, in particular, when one finds out the story of how this icon made it to the Monastery.

Irrespective the faith, or the god/s concept/s one believes in, the Shaghoura manifestation and presence, and what it represents, are real and deeply rooted in the psyche of humanity, especially, the manifested aura around this Monastery and its Shaghoura guardian. On some level, it is such iconic powers, such guardians of faith that guided and supported the choice of religion that is Christianity today, and they continue to prod worshippers with curiosity and anticipation as to how such powers of faith can be harnessed through their vows and offerings over the ages. Moreover, faith becomes a response to an unknown, the overwhelming unknowns related to death in the life of human beings, the what's next, the beyond-death unanswered questions. As such, faith becomes a choice to alleviate such anxieties, to make the journey simpler, to have a partner, a guardian, a strong shoulder to lean on, to make endings less harsh. The Shaghoura has attained such a status in my family, with all the support and spiritual dimensions its guardianship has provided my ancestors and family over centuries to date.

Shaghoura: The Story of an Icon

In the late eighth century, Abbess Marina asked Theodore, a Greek pilgrim monk from Egypt on his way to Jerusalem, to buy a precious icon of the Holy Virgin Mary from the Holy Land in Jerusalem and bring it back to the Monastery. After forgetting to buy the icon in Jerusalem, on his way back, an unfamiliar voice whispered in Theodore's ear and reminded him of Abbess Marina's request. Theodore returned to Jerusalem, found the icon of the Theotokos, and started on his journey back to the Monastery. It is believed that the icon he bought was one of four icons of the Holy Virgin Mary that St. Luke the Evangelist had painted. On the way back, the icon and the Holy Virgin Mary saved the caravan from bandits and wild beasts, and monk Theodore decided to keep the miraculous icon for himself and sail back to Egypt rather than head to Saydnaya. On the ship, before sailing off, a huge storm hit and the ship almost capsized. Theodore, overwhelmed with guilt and fear, left the ship, and went back to Saydnaya. At the Monastery, after spending four days there, he was tempted again to keep the icon and gave in to such temptations; he decided to leave with the icon hidden in his luggage. He apologized to Abbess Marina for not being able to find the requested icon, and tried to leave the Monastery secretly. At the Monastery's gate, an invisible energy with the strength of a stone wall blocked his way out. After several failed attempts to leave, Theodore finally handed the icon to Abbess Marina, told her of his journey back from Jerusalem, confessed his intentions and asked for her forgiveness. Abbess Marina was very moved by the unfolding of events and installed the icon inside the room, the room behind the Monastery's church and on the eastern wall of the Monastery, and the Shaghoura 'became', with all the miracles that ensued.

Amazing how our spiritual being, us terminal humans, can add a surreal dimension to our existence, within the earth journey, with guardians such as the Shaghoura and the bliss of vows being fulfilled. What an intense transformational dimension the mind can add to our lives with the belief structures and their impact on everyday life, on moments, on time — our time on earth...

The Monastery: Other Corners and Dwellings

The Reception: As soon as you arrive at the Monastery, the reception area near the office of the Abbess is the place of welcome, where nuns offer you coffee, tea, and water, and where you wait for the Abbess to come and welcome the group visiting. What immediately captures your attention in this large room are the pictures of past patriarchs and abbesses, mostly in black and white, hanging on the wall, high up, right above the seating area, striking and distinct. The intense looks on the faces of past abbesses are quite engaging, as if to speak of times past, conflicts past, moments past with eternal beings in the memory of the Monastery...

The Office: The office near the reception is where one pays the money associated with the vows, pays the offerings to the Monastery. It is also where the second Touma family vow is fulfilled, where one of the nuns cuts the hair of the young four-year-old boy and weighs the hair, before the parents donate the weight of the hair in gold to the Monastery. This is also where the nuns give the incense bags, the holy oil tubes, the small icons for rooms and cars, and the receipts for every fulfilled vow, per family.

The Shop: The shop is filled with icons of all shapes, sizes, and kinds: icons from Greece, Palestine, Lebanon, Syria, Egypt, and many other parts of the world... Entering this shop without buying something to cement one's fervor for and guardianship of the Shaghoura is near impossible to resist.

The Rest of the Monastery: I rarely visited or stayed in the

Monastery's library, kitchen, and bedrooms. But I can vouch for the nuns' hospitality and generosity. The built-up space of the Monastery is so old that one might take for granted electricity, internet connections, phone lines, and all the needed amenities in today's age... The look and aura of this Holy monument evokes the feeling, the assumption almost, that this Monastery is running on candles for eternity, to relive continuously the day it was built, relive the story, the history, all in the moment — wishful thinking, at best, but real energies nevertheless.

The Touma Family Journey

To fulfill the eternal vows my great grandfather made several decades back to the Lady of Saydnaya, the family transformed them into traditions, ceremonial in nature, thus bringing the family together for the ceremonious act of cutting a boy's hair or the baptism of a newly-born child, or just a visit to the Lady of Saydnaya Monastery.

Trip Preparations

For as long as I can remember, the trip to the Lady of Saydnaya Monastery was a family event par excellence... My father, my mother, my uncles and their wives, along with my grandmother, would fix both date and purpose of the pilgrimage, and initiate preparations.

On the day of the pilgrimage, the trip mobilization begins at three a.m., with all getting ready to make a move from our hometown in Kab-Elias in the Bekaa Valley towards the Monastery by four a.m. On the previous day, all families and our grandmother would have prepared food for the trip, including kibbeh (meat and cracked wheat), bread, cheese,

113

bread with thyme, bread with keshek (a cheese substitute), bread with meat, all kinds of sandwiches, all kinds of cakes, all kinds of fruits, water bottles, fruit juices, and cans of soft drink... Three to five cars loaded with the families and with enough food to feed over one hundred people...!

The Journey Begins

As we head towards the Monastery, the first stop is at the Lebanese border. The paperwork for all the family members is cleared within a few minutes, and while waiting, the devouring of all that food begins — as if we were all afraid of some sort of eternal famine striking our family for whatever absurd reason. With full stomachs, we cross the Lebanese border towards the Syrian border and fifteen minutes later, we reach Jdeidet Yabous, where a lot of other cars are waiting in long lines, and where a lot of paperwork needs to be processed. The feast resumes with eternal hunger striking each and every one of us... For whatever reason, eating becomes a key part of this vow-fulfilling journey, a communion with eating that all perform ceremoniously...

Maybe food was a way to avoid communication at such an early hour in the morning, avoid feeling awkward, avoid not being asleep... Oh well, watching the family feast again, and again, is not a sight easily forgotten.

We offer the guards at the border food, bread, and cigarettes as an expression of gratitude for facilitating the process... More than twenty-four people from the Touma family were crossing the border on that particular day... As the paperwork begins to clear, one car at a time, all coded by hand on papers and a pink booklet that each car has, without any computer systems, without any system to track us, or track our visits, or track the person entering or leaving... We begin crossing the border, and those who cross first wait for the rest, until all finish, and the convoy of cars is ready to mobilize, again... And all this in the early hours of morning, just as the dawn is starting to break.

The weather still very chilly, we continue on towards the Monastery, passing through several cities inside Syria, including the famous towns of Douma and Al Tall, until we reach the main road leading up to the town of Saydnaya and the Monastery. As we get closer, the roads become narrower and dangerous for two cars moving in opposite directions, let alone for a car and a truck...

Fear of such trucks is an understatement, but, for some reason, we would feel that the Shaghoura is protecting this convoy, and hence, all would be okay — or so we desperately wanted and needed to believe...

As we enter the town of Saydnaya, around seven a.m., my grandmother asks my father to stop so she can continue the journey on foot, barefoot, walking uphill to the Monastery.

It is a ten-minute walk and, for ten minutes, we all watch our grandmother move up the very steep hill, barefoot, probably repenting, probably performing one of her own vows, probably communicating in her own way with the Lady of Saydnaya, communicating with us, teaching us, communicating with her ancestors, with her pains, with her fears... How intense it was to watch a seventy-year-old woman, with one kidney, doing what she did, and all without explaining the whys of such a decision, such an act...

Let the Show Begin

We reach the Monastery, park the cars in front of the

115

stairway, open the trunks, and begin the food feast, again...
Sun up, it is breakfast time — supposedly, but for all the
Touma family, this is probably dinner time, three solid meals
within a three-hour period... Eating is part of the journey, an
undisclosed vow perhaps...

Finished with our food, we gather the needed paperwork
for the baptism/s, the needed clothes, the needed 'memory
log'... And we start the climb up the winding stairs towards
the front gate of the Monastery. My father and grandmother
enter first, chanting, praying, until we reach the reception area
of the Monastery. The Abbess greets us, and offers us coffee,
tea, and water, utterly unaware that we're all so full that even
oxygen would have a hard time entering our air passageways.

Finished with the welcome ritual, we move towards hair
cutting/s or baptism/s, depending on the vows 'scheduled for
fulfillment'. The hair cutting, weighing, and subsequent vow
payment are completed quite fast, all logged in the Book of the
Monastery in less than fifteen minutes...

The older boys watch on intently, with vivid memories of
their own vow surfacing, memories of their feelings as the
scissors chopped through their hair, as the nun's steady hand
moved across their head, as the noises that seemed never to
end continued, until they felt their head lighter, their memories
lighter, their pain of carrying the load of this vow that much
lighter...

On some level, our great grandfather knew what he was
doing and vow fulfillment is worthy of the celebration, of the
pain, of the eternal commitment associated with its
implementation.

The most anticipated vow was baptism...

The whole family made their way to the church where the

priest was waiting for us, with his long beard, and tall and towering body and demeanor... You could feel his inherent ability to terrorize the Satan he was about to kick out of the child's spirit, or so he would believe, and have us believe... With his deep voice, his minced words, this priest had performed so many baptisms that it almost feels like he just switches on his 'ritual implementation mode' without any recourse to memory, to books, to the bible, to anything — a machine unleashed...

As we start with the baptism motions and rituals, my parents, who were usually the godparents for most but their own children's baptisms, start praying. In his beautiful voice, my father starts chanting the very old Byzantine chants, awakening both walls and icons of the church, awakening the spirits of our ancestors, awakening all present to this eternal vow, awakening our consciousness of this moment, etching it in our souls to become a memorable vow for future generations, future nostalgic stories, future journeys...

The baptism is quick, violent, and mechanical...

One does not have time to reflect, to solemnly process what is happening; only the dominating voice echoing in one's head, the priest's voice which races through words with five sentences uttered in a mere few seconds, a speed of speech echoing his boredom, his readiness to be done with it, doing this ritual for money, for survival, without any spiritual value within, or so I felt — and on to the next one...

The baptism proceeds, and all I can recall is the child's terror, cries, fears, confusion surrounding their nakedness, their cold sensation, the water in the brass basin, and what was to come... The dramatic nature of the event and our heightened sensitivity to the child's vulnerability makes us all move with

117

the flow, anticipating the end with the cries of the child eternally present in the moment, in our ears, in our spirits...

Watching the baptism is not fun...

As the priest takes the child in his big hands, the child is engulfed, unnoticeable but for her/his cries, screams for help, screams for rescue from the priest's hands, and not necessarily from Satan...

Satan to the child was the priest, the sight of the water basin approaching, the three dives in the basin, the ever-present sounds and the melodic chants, the sight of her/his mother and father as the witnesses to such an event, not coming to her/his help, to rescue her/him from such a predicament — a drama for the child, a festive energy for the family watching, and a karma clearing event for the spirits past, for our great grandfather in particular... What a feast for the senses, for the ages, for memories past, for young and old to remember, to move past, to transcend, and repeat again, when the vow is there to fulfill...

Finished with the baptism, with the spitting on evil, with the triumph over Satan, with the rebirth, with the seal of belonging and the holy Myron, with the eternal vow fulfillment, the family, along with the newly baptized child or children, move to the Shaghoura for the most intense prayer modes I have ever seen in my life.

When we enter the candle-lit sacred room where the Shaghoura is, the reverence the family holds for such an event is felt so intensely it is almost tangible. The family fills the sacred Shaghoura half-circular room, praying, listening, observing, following the prayer rhythm of the nun leading the ritual, candles lighting up their solemn faces, their souls, their fears, their wishes, their questions, their introspective spirits, deeply moved, and deeply silent within... Each family member, standing barefoot, engrossed and absorbed in their own thoughts, communicating with God, with the Holy Virgin Mary, with their conscience, with their pain, with their journeys ahead... Oh what a series of inner family journeys these were while growing up...

The Journey Ends

After the Shaghoura visit, certain family members visit the Monastery shop to buy nostalgic ornaments, icons, memory-markers for sentimental inner trips, if any... Moreover, the Abbess offers the families ample blessed small oil containers, small bags of incense with olive tree leaves, icons for cars, offices, homes, and hand ribbons for all to wear.

Done with the visits, with the chanting, with the church touring, again and again, done with the trips within and along the spiritual edge, the family starts preparations for going back home, back to reality, to Kab-Elias.

Again, as soon as we go down the stairs of the Monastery, approach the cars, the eternal famine fears take over, and with this unspoken awareness, this implicit consensus, we eat... again...

The mystery of such eating ceremonies still escapes me, but the rhythm of the ceremony never did. Unreservedly endearing and so surreal in their manifestations in my memory as I write these words... What was it? The food? The abundance of it? The fear of hunger? Fear of death? Reaffirmation of life while combating Satan and supposedly prevailing? Eternal screams to the ancestors, with chants of karmic cleansing, chants of eternal vow-clearance, chants of forgiveness to those harmed by our ancestors, by their actions, or maybe our actions…?

Food marks a new beginning, a new start, a new communion, a new chapter… Together, as a family, like we were when we were kids, food washes tension and clears the hate or resentment deep within the soul, deep within the family psyche, deep and hidden from sight, and fully transparent with the food feasts along the way…

On the journey back, we stop a few times to buy ice cream, walnuts, dried nuts, dried figs and raisins, and, at times, Damascus sweets from the Al Hamidieh Souks… Those souks were memorable, massive, impressive, and quite a treat should the family decide to stop.

The journey back home would always feel longer, the time longer, the wait longer, and the anticipation to arrive almost omnipresent. We stop at the Syrian border, we get checked by the security guards, get asked many questions, and without any resistance we respond, just wanting to finish and be done with it…

The funniest moment was always at the Lebanese border when one of the mothers, or fathers, or our grandmother would ask if anyone was hungry, if we wanted anything to eat along the way! As if we did not have enough!

I guess the soul-filling experience of the Monastery visit would never be enough to sustain us… Food would always appease the pain and instill a sense of serenity, of fullness, of satiation, contemplating tomorrow, and anticipating the next trip, tickled by the fun of the gathered family, all united in homage to the Lady of Saydnaya, in homage to the memory of our ancestors, in homage to the karmic cleansing that took place that day, in homage to the eternal vows and communion with both past and present, all in one day, one visit, and many more since…

Notes…

Family karma is a cycle we ride simply by being part of the family, eternally looping, a cycle that we may not be responsible for initiating, but whose effects and repercussions most certainly impact us. The loop of life, of karma, is something we are eternally tied to when we are part of a family. It comes with its positives and negatives and is inescapable. One can choose to leave a family, separate from it, but one cannot break free from the ancestors' karma and its enduring impact on her/him and her/his family, and the global family lineage.

In Buddhism, self-realization is fulfilled with prayers and work… In my family, my self-realization has been attained through the vows and pilgrimages to the Lady of Saydnaya Monastery, and the work legacy I inherited from my father before he passed. Does it suit me now, at my age, to move forward with the karma I inherited? For sure yes, as I find it very endearing, and, on some level, I am playing my role in getting such karma cleared, all while dancing with life, and making the best of the cards I am dealt.

My Journey

When we grow older and understand the meaning of such vows, we accept their power and significance, and we move towards implementation with solid footing, not caring about the interpretation — in the moment — of our children, our spouse, our in-laws… with a sole focus of fulfilling the vows, not daring to allow alternatives or logical reasonings as to 'hows' or 'why nots' to surface, not daring to contemplate new forms of karma clearing. Deep down, I was most likely concerned for my children from the retribution of my ancestors, afraid of my own guilt, troubled by my own 'what ifs'... Were the fears justified? Definitely not, but I entertained them nonetheless, with nostalgia and within our momentary existence. For sure I wanted to modify the traumatic cycle of baptism, but my nostalgic memory was stronger, wanting to repeat what I saw growing up, wanting to relive those past and long-gone moments at the same place, with the same vows...

My wife and I are blessed with one daughter and two sons. Their journeys to the Lady of Saydnaya Monastery were anything but ordinary.

Our Daughter

Our daughter was the first granddaughter born into my father's family, and, as expected, there was a lot of anticipation for implementing the first vow of baptism when she turned nine months old in May, 1999... This also marked the first baptism since my father's passing in 1994, and, as such, a communion with him, his legacy, his first grandchild going through the mill of the cycle of vow fulfillment, the family committed to this trip that represented so much, held so much, and meant so much... Getting the family rallied, preparing the food, organizing the drivers and the cars, and mobilizing toward the Lady of Saydnaya Monastery was a major feat.

At the Monastery, we go through the regular ritual: reception, office, church, baptism, Shaghoura, and back... During the baptism, the most striking energies of fear and emotional distress were those of my wife and her mother, who never witnessed such a violent immersion and Satan exorcism before... They were both crying, and both very angry at the

122

priest for being so vengeful in his execution of what was, supposedly, a simple baptism process. On our way back, the first question from both my wife and her mother asked was whether we had the option to avoid the vow fulfillment at the Monastery with future children, and my response was a categoric 'No'... Their shock was completely expected and I assumed they would get used to such 'violence' over time — or so I hoped...

Our Oldest Son

During the summer of 2005, our oldest son's baptism was smooth. The most disturbing event was the cavalier manner in which the priest flipped our son and threw him at the godfather (my older brother) after the three immersions. We were all shocked at what resembled a show of gymnastics or a stunt in the circus... The family members filmed this event, and the screams of shock were an understatement. Should we assume the priest was practicing such moves before we came? Should we assume it was entertaining for the priest who was overcome with the boredom of repetition and needed to amp things up a little? All assumptions and no certainties, none other than the anger I felt... As far as my wife and her mother are concerned, no assumptions needed to be made; their bulging eyes, fear-filled expressions and screams of caution said it all...

Again, my great grandfather must have been happy with such karma clearance — so I sarcastically assume...

In December of 2008, my oldest son turned four and so it was time to fulfill the second vow. Soon after celebrating his birthday, a small group of the Touma family lineage gathered early in Chtaura, Bekaa Valley, and we made our way to the Monastery. It was a simple and quick visit. Upon reaching the office in the Monastery, panic set in; it was the first hair-cutting vow fulfillment in my family and my wife and I weren't quite sure what to expect, how our young son, with his hair pulled back in a pony tail, would react, how we would react.

Despite all the verbal preparations and thorough explanations, nothing could explain the vow's eventful implementation to a four-year-old child... As the nun started praying and cutting our son's hair, we all stopped breathing, and he froze, motionless, waiting, cringing, scared, and full of anticipation of the freedom awaiting him, freedom from his girl-like looks, from the hair that was too hard to wash, brush, carry, sleep with, be with... When the nun finished, we screamed with joy, while our son cried with anguish, silently, intently, touching his head, watching the hair on the weight scale, watching me donate to the Monastery the weight of his hair in gold — still crying, still wanting his hair to last a bit longer, the Samson hair... or so we thought...

It was very touching watching my boy lose part of his 'body', part of his look, part of his history on this earth, all of a sudden, all in the name of a vow he had nothing to do with, a vow he could not refuse... A very emotional day for me, to this day...

My wife kept the hair in a paper envelope and brought it back for memories, for the logged time and care in each and every braid, for our son's nostalgic journeys back to the Monastery with his kids in the future...

Our Youngest Son

Our youngest son was born in 2012, eight years after his brother, fourteen years after his sister, during the Syrian war, with all roads blocked in 2013 to the Lady of Saydnaya Monastery, with the Monastery getting bombed, and with many risks involved in getting in and out of Syria during that period.

His baptism had to be postponed, with all my anxieties, with all my guilt, with all my fears of angering the legacy of my ancestors, the Touma family legacy… Delaying the baptism was not a choice, as it was too risky to gather the whole family, and just go…

The first year passed, and the nuns called my wife and me and asked us to come. On several occasions they offered to send the Monastery's driver and car to come pick us up. My wife refused. The second year passed, and the third year passed, and we could not go to the Monastery, and our son was still not baptized. Baptizing him in Lebanon was not an option, as such this vow needed to be performed at the Lady of Saydnaya Monastery and no other church would do. The hair-cutting, on the other hand, could be done in Lebanon, by the nuns of the Monastery, if needed.

On September seventh, 2016, our son turned four, and it was time to cut his hair. Still not baptized, we called the nuns at the Monastery and they were very confident the roads were safe for our visit. That same week after our son's fourth birthday, my wife and I decided to head to Saydnaya, perform both vows in one trip, and with only our immediate family members, the five of us, making the journey. We felt it unfair to ask any other family member to join us and risk their safety given that Syria was still going through a ravaging war. Once decided, we called the Monastery, requested they send the Monastery's car and driver to pick us up from Chtaura, Bekaa Valley, in September 2016.

Mind made up, we head out to the Monastery at six a.m., crossing more than twelve road blocks, with army, secret services, and internal security stop points, with all kinds of checking, searching, and digging through the luggage and food we had, and in the car we were in… The journey took three hours, but all so worth it, after such an anticipated reunion and pilgrimage.

I could not wait to get the load of the vows off my heart, my mind, my conscience, my karma…

We arrive at the Monastery, after a long absence that lasted years since the war started. We calmly go up the winding stairs, with all memories coming back, and itching away at us during the climb. There was no one else visiting the Monastery on that particular day. The Monastery felt sad and a bit eerie that morning, at nine a.m. The Syrian war had taken its toll on the Monastery, and it was obvious…

The nuns were expecting us. Once we entered the gate, the Abbess welcomed us in front of the church, and we went up to the reception area for some refreshments and to plan the baptism as we did not have a godmother or godfather…

When I asked the Abbess to be the godmother, she immediately said no, suggesting that we chose someone to be with our son as he grows older, be with him as his godmother. And when she recommended our daughter, our son's eighteen-year-old sister to be the godmother, our faces lit up and we all started crying! We were flabbergasted… The Abbess went on to recommend our oldest son, his twelve-year-old brother, be his godfather, chaperoned by a senior nun until our oldest son reached eighteen years of age… Another shock and oh so very endearing to all of us… Our son's sister and brother as his godparents, and all within the surreal setting of a war decision, a war baptism, a war vow fulfillment, under the most unstable of circumstances.

The plan decided, we proceeded with the motions of the baptism, all while realizing that our youngest son is a strong, tall, four-year-old, and not a small nine-month-old child... The priest was very violent, as usual, and our son cried profusely during and after the baptism, looking at us with bitter eyes, questioning eyes as to why we let this happen to him.

The godparents, along with the nun, were there, helping out, going through the motions and making the baptism happen, as quickly as possible.

Our oldest son was crying and sad, sad with the knowledge that his brother was old enough to remember such violence perpetrated on him, to remember those moments, moments too forceful on his brother's spirit...

No matter what, we could not explain to both our sons, aged twelve and four, the value of this vow, and the need for it to take place. We were sad they were both crying, but our tears, my wife's and mine, were tears of joy because we were performing a vow that was, by that time, delayed for over three years.

After dressing our newly baptized son with new and fresh clothes, we went up to the office, where the Abbess was waiting for us to cut his hair. Our youngest son, still angry, was sitting peacefully on the desk, in the office, surrounded by the nuns, by his godparents, by his parents... The Abbess begins the cutting, while all of us are crying at the sight of this rite of passage, this vow being performed, this eternal cry to the gods for helping us through it, to our ancestors for making us move with it, irrespective of the risks, irrespective of my wife's and my earlier trepidations.

We weigh the hair, donate its weight in gold, and show our son his hair. He is watching, still observing, not understanding, not caring, just wanting this assault on his body and his system to be over… Again, my wife packs the hair in a paper envelope to bring back with us…

We all kissed and hugged, glad that is was all over, blessed that we could do it on time, blessed that the vows were fulfilled, in spite of such a damaging war on both Monastery and Syria.

We visit the Shaghoura, and soon after, we start hearing airplanes bombing the town of Douma, fifteen minutes away from the Monastery.

At eleven a.m., the nuns ask us to stay for lunch, but we politely decline the offer, call the driver to join us at the parking of the Monastery, and head back to Lebanon for the three-hour journey back to Chtaura.

On our way back, I had a million thoughts going through my head, fears, trepidations, anticipations of airplanes bombing the roads on our journey back — all kinds of anxieties, until we reached the border.

I've never felt such an extreme sense of relief as I did that day… Relieved that we got the centuries-old vows executed, peacefully… And so touched that our youngest son has his older sister and brother as his godparents… How surreal, how sweet, how serene, how eternally powerful for their journey together, for their love for each other, for their adoption of their younger brother going forward… Eternally grateful is an understatement…

Final Thoughts

When one analyses Christianity on a much deeper level, one senses an obsession with the concept of virginity and the immaculate conception, the virgin mythology, cleanliness, water, oil, light, east, sacred rituals to bond and move the masses... Evil, Satan, death, and after-death are but ways to control the masses, and to move them in directions that the Church desires, and make of them flocking birds inside the nest of faith, from baptism to burial... Baptism, death, resurrection, and the eternal journey are intertwined with all the makeup of the pillars of the Christian faith... Christ's resurrection is core in Christianity as it gives hope to the faithful, hope with eternity, communion with what's next, hope that life continues after their death, with them in it, a player, an actor, a witness... Fake hope at best, but while the journey is unfolding, the pain of finality is that much appeased with such beliefs — for a while at least...

Ya Shaghoura... An eternal cry, scream, breath, call to action, call for help you so are, the Shaghoura of my great grandfather and his family... Shaghoura, you are the logger of moments, of memories, of screams for help, of eternal forgiveness, of eternal penitence... I bid you peace as you have been such an omnipresent force and spirit in our lives... You have brought us together, you have united us against the 'evil' within and outside of us, you have made us whole in getting such karma vows cleared... Be they temporary in time, such karma vows are eternal for the family to be one with its deeds, its actions, its conscience, its present, its past, and hopefully, its future...

O Shaghoura... How I miss you, and miss my late father and uncles within what remains of such memories, moments gone, and yet eternal with our remembering them now, documenting such memories now, trying to make memories live through us and with us, albeit for a tender and sweet moment, albeit faintly, but very real nevertheless... As for me, I am sitting here, waiting for my family members to remember my wife and me and our ancestors one day as they experience their own personal journeys with the family vows...

To my ancestors, I bid you all serenity, as, for now, the vows, or shall we call them the great grandfather karma vows, have been cleared for all your and our children, and for many generations to come... Or so we, you, and your spirits hope...

My great grandfather, your karmic cycle lives on, with eternal rage it lives on... It lives on inside each one of us, inescapable, forever present, reminding us, calling upon us to act...

Until we meet, my dear ancestors... I bid you peace... I do so hope...

for accepting the end of boyhood in my son, for accepting the eternal goodbyes...

I have never forgotten how I felt that day, and probably never will.

To My Son

I bid you peace my boy, my son... I love you more than you could fathom and ask you to forgive me if I ever treated you with my own selfishness, treated you brutally with my own existential struggle, treated you with my rejection of my end, my end around you, my end in your life...

Please forgive this old and weak man who is your father, struggling to let you go, struggling to let himself go, to exit...

I bid me peace my son, because I am going to need it, badly... and sadly...

The Smart Middle

Many times in life, we allow ourselves to get close to certain individuals. But too much closeness always comes at a price: expectations increase drastically, communication becomes too personal, interventions in each other's lives become the norm, and the privacy of each person becomes optional.

And such relationships probably started as simple acquaintances, simple friendships, simple get-togethers. Why we allow such relationships to get too close is always a personal choice, a decision we make, a premeditated act that we pursue. In the midst and in the depth of such an interaction, taking a step back becomes difficult and might lead to separation conflicts, blame games, manipulations — be they emotional or mental... Simply put, bringing such closeness back to a balanced state of friendship is no easy task, it makes the engagements forward too difficult and may lead to a violent rupture of this close friendship that has pushed the boundaries of a healthy human connection...

Mind you, such violent ruptures are not simple to manage, can be hard to swallow, and will most probably cause deep internal conflicts and guilt trips with oneself: "Did I do the right thing? Why did I let it reach this level? Why wasn't I more tolerant?" Moreover, such ruptures can lead to blame games with one's partner where the expectation of the partner preventing us from being in such a predicament in the first place is exposed, revealed… It's much simpler to blame our own actions, actions that led to this 'too close' relationship, rather than justify them in terms of our own inability to find a smart and healthy middle… And last, after several months of separation, the rupture gives us a sense of freedom from the load this relationship was, and allows us to breathe better — all because we allowed the interactions to get too close for our own comfort and the relationship to become a heavy burden to carry rather than an enriching encounter to seek and nurture…

Smart Middle: Find It

The obvious people to get too close to are: parents, siblings, friends, children, business partners, neighbors, colleagues, parents of our children's friends, prayer/yoga/sports partners, and the list goes on… The problem with all the above is that we cannot easily make a clean-cut separation from such individuals if we get too close, if we do not respect the smart middle between us. Even putting limits on such relationships becomes too difficult, fraught with many kinds of expectations and manipulations that either party can pressure the other one into.

Friends are great for our wellbeing, and family provides us a solid support infrastructure that we have to appreciate. But to avoid such conflicts and potential ruptures one has to respect the smart middle. The smart middle is where we get close enough, but not too close, and far enough, but not too far. The smart middle is where we limit our closeness to subtle interventions, unassuming questions, simple gatherings, casual get-togethers, true but not conflicted conversations, peaceful encounters planned ahead and without high expectations — all with a controlled frequency per encounter and type of encounter. A high frequency will force the encroachment on privacy, as the usual, typical, surface-level, non-invasive topics would have been covered, and the conversations will delve into the personal, and hence, break the smart middle, and its benefits in maintaining the light nature of the friendship.

Smart Middle: The Art

Finding the smart middle is an art as it is unique for every person, family member, or friend. More importantly, the smart middle is an attitude towards relationships in general. We have to constantly be aware of where the boundaries of this middle are, and when they are crossed. Through laziness and manipulations, very frequent encounters, unawareness and vulnerability, the smart middle can easily be crossed by close family members and/or friends without our conscious consent, and without our awareness at times. Such crossing can be due to the absence of meaning in the life of the friend or family member. Such lack of meaning can erase such smart middle, push such a relationship into our realm of privacy, and steal our meaning, our inner peace, our inner calm, just because it makes the other party feel better.

As such, the smart middle is where we stay vigilant about our inner calm, inner sanctum, and protect our meaning and our friendships, without resorting to pushing them away or ridding ourselves of them.

Such vigilance comes from awareness, from the fact that we cannot rid ourselves of family, and from the fact that we